Workbook

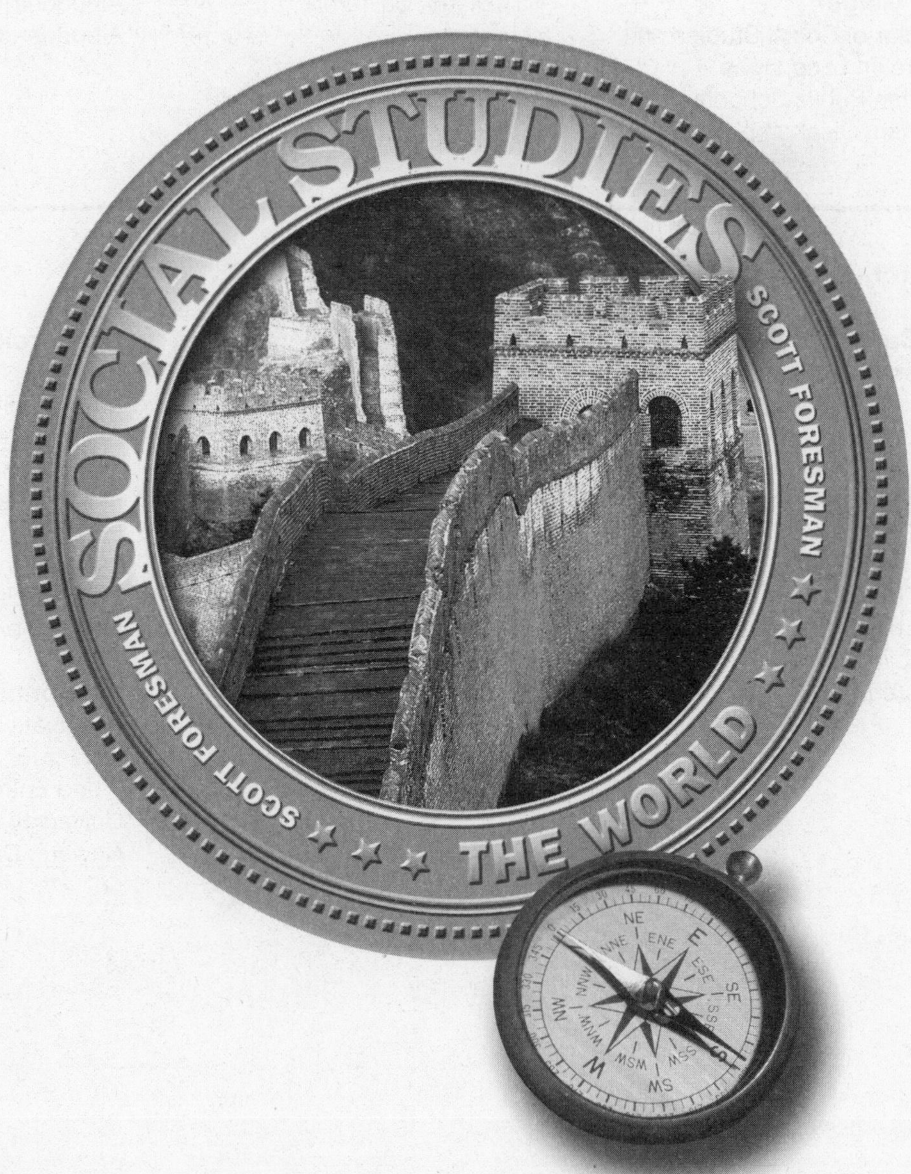

Editorial Offices: Glenview, Illinois • Parsippany, New Jersey • New York, New York
Sales Offices: Parsippany, New Jersey • Duluth, Georgia • Glenview, Illinois
Coppell, Texas • Ontario, California • Mesa, Arizona

www.sfsocialstudies.com

Program Authors

Dr. Candy Dawson Boyd
Professor, School of Education
Director of Reading Programs
St. Mary's College
Moraga, California

Dr. Geneva Gay
Professor of Education
University of Washington
Seattle, Washington

Rita Geiger
Director of Social Studies and Foreign Languages
Norman Public Schools
Norman, Oklahoma

Dr. James B. Kracht
Associate Dean for Undergraduate Programs and Teacher Education
College of Education
Texas A & M University
College Station, Texas

Dr. Valerie Ooka Pang
Professor of Teacher Education
San Diego State University
San Diego, California

Dr. C. Frederick Risinger
Director, Professional Development and Social Studies Education
Indiana University
Bloomington, Indiana

Sara Miranda Sanchez
Elementary and Early Childhood Curriculum Coordinator
Albuquerque Public Schools
Albuquerque, New Mexico

Contributing Authors

Dr. Carol Berkin
Professor of History
Baruch College and the Graduate Center
The City University of New York
New York, New York

Lee A. Chase
Staff Development Specialist
Chesterfield County Public Schools
Chesterfield County, Virginia

Dr. Jim Cummins
Professor of Curriculum
Ontario Institute for Studies in Education
University of Toronto
Toronto, Canada

Dr. Allen D. Glenn
Professor and Dean Emeritus
College of Education
Curriculum and Instruction
University of Washington
Seattle, Washington

Dr. Carole L. Hahn
Professor, Educational Studies
Emory University
Atlanta, Georgia

Dr. M. Gail Hickey
Professor of Education
Indiana University-Purdue University
Ft. Wayne, Indiana

Dr. Bonnie Meszaros
Associate Director
Center for Economic Education and Entrepreneurship
University of Delaware
Newark, Delaware

ISBN 0-328-08181-7

15-V004-13 12 11

Contents

Name ______________________ Date ______________ **Reading Social Studies**

Use with Pages 6–7.

Sequence

Sequence refers to the order in which events occur. Sometimes writers use clue words such as *first, next, after,* and *finally* to signal sequence.

Directions: Read the following passage. Then fill in the circle next to the correct answer.

Ancestors of the Pueblo used a technique called coiling to make baskets. Coiling uses two pieces of material—the foundation and the wrapping strip.

During prehistoric times, a basket maker might have followed a sequence similar to the one below to make a coiled basket.

The basket maker first determines the purpose for the basket. Knowing this helps him or her figure out the size of the basket and how much material will be needed to make it. Then the basket maker decides if a pattern is wanted. If so, certain colors will be considered when choosing materials. Next, suitable materials are gathered in adequate amounts. The materials needed for the foundation are different from those needed for the wrapping strip.

After choosing and obtaining the materials, the basket maker gets started. The starting point is the center of the bottom of the basket. The foundation, which consists of many long, thin fibers, is gathered together. It is then coiled spirally in a circle. The circle is held together with the wrapping strip, which binds each coil to the one before it. This makes a flat surface. Once the base of the basket is as wide as is needed, it's time to start working on the sides. To make the sides, the coils are bound, one on top of another, with the wrapping strip.

1. What is the first thing a basket maker should do?

Ⓐ obtain the materials for the basket
Ⓑ determine the purpose for the basket
Ⓒ decide the pattern of the basket
Ⓓ choose a color for the basket

2. When should you decide if a pattern is wanted?

Ⓐ before you determine the purpose of the basket
Ⓑ after obtaining the materials
Ⓒ after you determine the purpose of the basket
Ⓓ after you make the base

3. Which part of the basket is worked on first?

Ⓐ the bottom
Ⓑ the wrapping strip
Ⓒ the sides
Ⓓ the top

Notes for Home: Your child learned about sequencing events.
Home Activity: With your child, take narrow strips of newspaper or cloth and weave a simple mat. Weave each strip by alternately going over and then under the other strips. Point out the importance of following the over-under sequence. Ask your child what might happen if the proper sequence of steps is not followed when weaving the mat.

Name ______________________ Date ____________ **Vocabulary Preview**

Use with Chapter 1.

Vocabulary Preview

Directions: Match each vocabulary word to its meaning. Write the number of the vocabulary word on the line before the definition. You may use your glossary. Not all words are used.

1. prehistory
2. archaeology
3. archaeologist
4. artifact
5. migrate
6. glacier
7. technology
8. domesticate
9. harvest
10. excavation site
11. agriculture
12. surplus
13. nomad
14. social division
15. climate
16. carbon dating
17. culture
18. landform
19. geography
20. diverse

_______ **a.** the study of the ways of past cultures through objects they left behind

_______ **b.** way in which humans produce the items they use

_______ **c.** the technology, customs, beliefs, and art of a group of people

_______ **d.** to tame wild animals or plants

_______ **e.** extra supply

_______ **f.** the study of the relationship between physical features, climate, and people

_______ **g.** an area's average weather conditions over a long span of time

_______ **h.** an object made by people long ago

_______ **i.** a huge sheet of ice covering a great stretch of land

_______ **j.** a surface feature such as a valley, plain, hill, or mountain

_______ **k.** place where archaeologists dig up artifacts

_______ **l.** to move from one area to another

_______ **m.** one who carefully uncovers evidence from the past

_______ **n.** a method scientists use to estimate the age of living things after they have died

_______ **o.** to gather

_______ **p.** a long period of time before people developed systems of writing and written language

_______ **q.** a person who travels from place to place

Notes for Home: Your child learned the vocabulary words for Chapter 1.
Home Activity: With your child, write the vocabulary words on index cards or pieces of paper. Have your child choose a word card at random and use the word in a sentence that relates to ancient civilizations.

Name ______________________ Date __________

Lesson Review

Use with Pages 10–16.

Lesson 1: Early Gatherers and Hunters

Directions: Use the terms in the box to complete each sentence with information from Lesson 1. Some terms will be used more than once.

artifacts	ancient	Clovis	hunters	Americans
archaeology	migrated	Ice Age	land bridge	archaeologists

1. ______________ is the science of studying past cultures through objects they left behind.
2. Tools, weapons, and jewelry are examples of ______________.
3. Archaeologists are interested not only in ______________, such as bone sewing needles, but also in anything else, such as bones left behind from a meal, that will give them clues about ancient cultures.
4. An archaeologist's job is to draw conclusions about the daily lives of ______________ peoples.
5. Some scholars believe that early peoples ______________ from East Africa to Asia and Europe thousands of years ago.
6. About 70 years ago, human-made objects that were approximately 11,000 years old were discovered in ______________, New Mexico.
7. The ______________ lasted until about 10,000 years ago.
8. One scientific theory states that Beringia, now called the Bering Strait, became a ______________ when the seas were low during the Ice Age.
9. Scientists believe that ______________ followed animals across the land bridge between Asia and North America.
10. For years, scholars believed that the first ______________ were the Clovis people of 11,000 years ago.
11. Some ______________ refused to accept the idea that artifacts found in Chile predate those they once believed were left behind by the first Americans.

Notes for Home: Your child learned about early cultures and how we study them.
Home Activity: With your child, make a chart with two columns. In one column, list artifacts that can be found in your home. In the other column, list what an archaeologist of the future might conclude about your lifestyle after examining these artifacts.

Name ______________________ Date __________ **Lesson Review**

Use with Pages 18–23.

Lesson 2: Early Farmers

Directions: Write *True* or *False* for each sentence. If the statement is false, rewrite it to make it true. You may use your textbook.

1. The two parts of the Stone Age are the Old Stone Age and the Prehistoric Stone Age.

   ____

2. A great deal of progress was made during the Old Stone Age.

   ____

3. Archaeologists piece together artifacts and other information about prehistoric times to better understand life long ago.

   ____

4. The discovery of metals and the development of metalworking mark the beginning of the New Stone Age.

   ____

5. Humans had to wait for glaciers to spread before they could begin growing crops.

   ____

6. The first plants to be domesticated were grasses.

   ____

7. Domestication of plants lasted only during the Stone Age.

   ____

8. Humans realized that animals could be useful and began to domesticate them.

   ____

9. Animals did not contribute to the development of agriculture.

   ____

10. Animals such as donkeys and camels were used to move people and goods.

    ____

Notes for Home: Your child learned about early farming practices.
Home Activity: With your child, brainstorm a list of ways that modern technology is used on farms today. Then discuss which elements of ancient farming still exist in the United States. Which still exist in less-developed nations? How have U.S. farmers improved their technology?

Name ______________________ Date ____________ **Chart and Graph Skills**

Use with Pages 24–25.

Use Parallel Time Lines

Directions: The parallel time lines on pp. 24–25 of your textbook are horizontal. Parallel time lines also can be vertical. Look at the vertical time lines on this page. Notice the dates and events each time line represents. Now look at the events in the box. Sequence them on the correct time line. Draw a line at the correct date and then write the events on the time line.

c. 2 million B.C.: First stone tools made from pebbles
c. 40,000 B.C.: Rock engravings in Australia
c. 24,000 B.C.: Cave paintings in Africa
c. 17,000 B.C.: Cave paintings in France and Spain
c. 12,000 B.C.: Bison painting in Spain
c. 10,000 B.C.: Variety of stone tools
c. 8,000 B.C.: Stone hoes and sickles
c. 5,500 B.C.: Cave painting in Algeria
c. 5,000 B.C.: Metal tools
c. 3,000 B.C.: Bronze tools

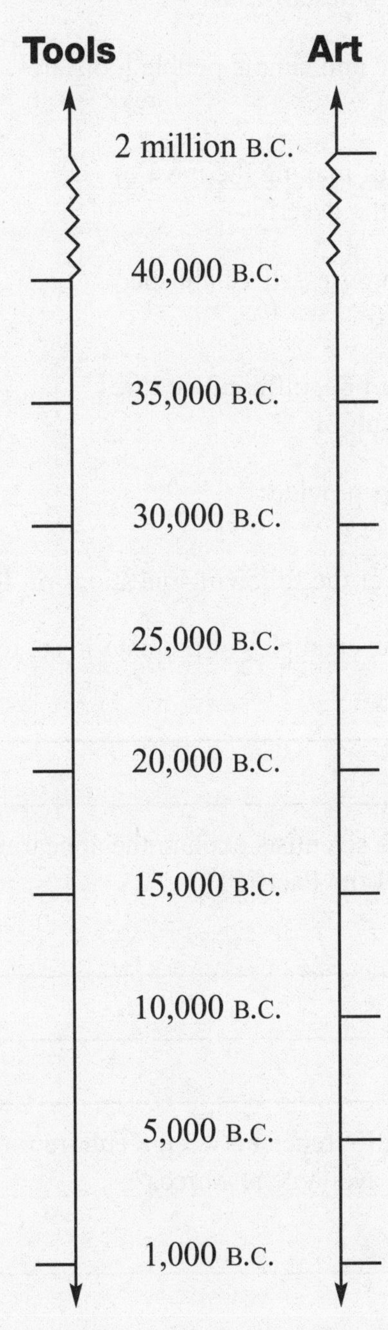

Notes for Home: Your child learned to read and use parallel time lines.
Home Activity: With your child, make parallel time lines for tomorrow's activities scheduled for you and your child.

Name ________________________ Date ____________ **Lesson Review**

Use with Pages 26–29.

Lesson 3: Developing Cultures

Directions: Draw a line from each item in Column A to the word or phrase in Column B that best completes the sentence.

Column A

1. Culture can be described as
2. Ancient stone and simple pebble tools are indications of
3. An example of making the most of resources in the desert is
4. As cultures progressed, established farming led to
5. In ancient Europe, different cultures arose as a result of
6. Prehistoric art provides

Column B

a. the variety of landforms, climates, and types of soil.

b. the way in which individuals and groups interact with their environment.

c. a valuable view of the prehistoric world.

d. settlements.

e. a Stone Age culture.

f. people making twine, nets, baskets, and other items from plant stems or fibers.

Directions: Answer the following questions on the lines provided.

7. Why are some examples of prehistoric art in France and Spain so well preserved?

____

____

8. How do some scientists explain the appearance of the sweet potato in both the Americas and islands of the Pacific?

____

____

____

9. What is one difference between a culture today using available resources and a prehistoric culture using available resources?

____

____

Notes for Home: Your child learned about the development of early cultures.
Home Activity: With your child, discuss how the availability of resources had a great effect on the way cultures developed. Together, look at a map of your home state or region. Point to areas with different geographical features and ask how those features might have affected a culture's development. Discuss what types of resources are unique to certain areas and what resources are common to most areas.

Name ______________________ Date ____________ **Vocabulary Review**

Use with Chapter 1.

Vocabulary Review

Directions: Use the clues from Chapter 1 to complete the crossword puzzle.

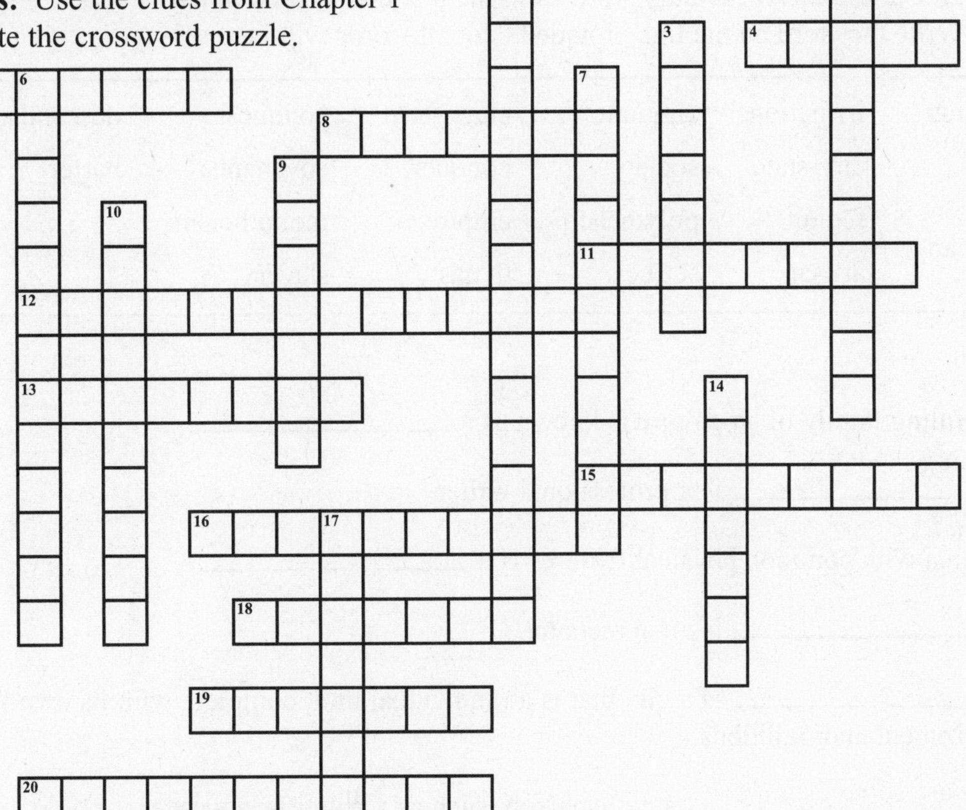

Across

4. person who travels from place to place
5. _____ dating method used to estimate age after something dies
8. huge ice sheet covering a stretch of land
11. object made by people long ago
12. place where archaeologists dig up artifacts
13. surface feature such as a valley or hill
15. the study of the relationship between physical features, climate, and people
16. long period of time before people developed systems of writing and a written language
18. extra supply
19. different
20. the raising of plants and animals

Down

1. to tame wild animals and plants
2. formed when work was divided up among villagers
3. average weather conditions over time
6. one who carefully uncovers evidence from the past
7. the study of the ways of life of early people through things they left behind
9. the technology, customs, beliefs, and art of a people
10. way in which humans produce the items they use
14. to move from one area to another
17. to gather

Notes for Home: Your child learned about early civilizations.
Home Activity: Ask your child to tell you about the job of an archaeologist. Have your child use as many of the vocabulary words as possible in his or her description.

Name ____________________ Date ____________

Vocabulary Preview

Use with Chapter 2.

Vocabulary Preview

Directions: Choose the vocabulary word from the box that best completes each sentence. Write the word on the line provided. Not all words will be used.

civilization	irrigation	ziggurat	cuneiform	conquest	descendant
fertile	city-state	society	conquer	covenant	barter
plain	region	polytheism	empire	monotheism	
plateau	artisan	scribe	dynasty	slavery	

1. The ruling family of an empire is known as a ____________.

2. A ____________ is a professional writer.

3. An area with common physical features is a ____________.

4. A ____________ is an agreement.

5. A ____________ is a city that is an individual unit, complete with its own form of government and traditions.

6. An ____________ is a craftsperson, such as a potter or a weaver.

7. To ____________ is to exchange goods and services.

8. A ____________ is an area of high, flat land.

9. A ____________ is a huge pyramid-shaped structure formed from a series of stacked rectangular platforms.

10. The practice of worshipping only one God is called ____________.

11. To worship many gods is to practice ____________.

12. A group of people who have a complex, organized society is called a ____________.

13. An ____________ is a large territory consisting of many places all under the control of a single ruler.

14. The practice of one person owning another person is known as ____________.

Notes for Home: Your child learned the vocabulary words for Chapter 2.
Home Activity: With your child, use each vocabulary word in a sentence.

Name ______________________ Date __________

Lesson Review

Use with Pages 34–39.

Lesson 1: The Fertile Crescent

Directions: Read the passage. Write the main idea and the details in the boxes.

Around the year 3500 B.C., one of the first civilizations began in a region known today as the Fertile Crescent. The center part of the Fertile Crescent is a land known as Mesopotamia.

Mesopotamia lies between two rivers, the Tigris and Euphrates. In fact, the word Mesopotamia means "the land between the rivers." These rivers played an important role in the civilization that developed there.

The people who lived in Mesopotamia had to overcome many obstacles in order to survive. The climate in this part of the world did not make farming easy. During the extremely hot summers, the land was very dry. During the rainy season, the rivers flooded the land. Natural resources were limited to little more than water and soil. There were few trees to provide wood for construction and other uses.

Fortunately, the people were good problem solvers. They designed an irrigation system that brought water from the rivers to their fields. This system allowed them to grow crops such as straw. By mixing the straw with mud, they were able to make bricks for building shelters.

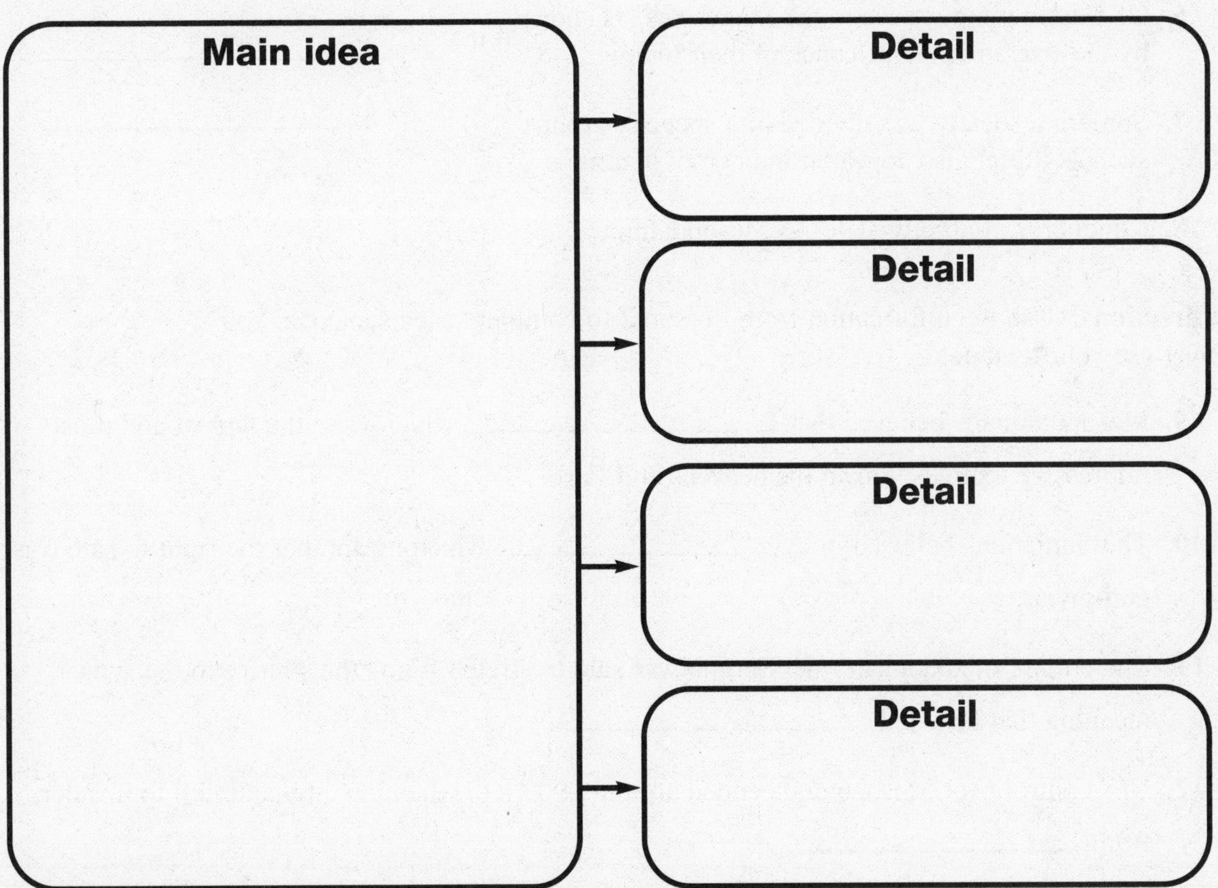

Notes for Home: Your child learned about one of the first civilizations.

Home Activity: Ask your child to identify the main idea and details of a favorite story or book. You may wish to make a chart similar to the one shown in this lesson and complete it together.

Name ______________________ Date __________ **Lesson Review**

Use with Pages 40–46.

Lesson 2: Mesopotamia

Directions: Match the terms in the box to the clues. Write the terms on the lines provided. You may use your textbook.

Akkad	class system	religion	Sumer
Akkadian	mudbrick wall	Sargon	Sumerian

1. City-state in northern Mesopotamia — 1. ____________
2. City-state in southern Mesopotamia — 2. ____________
3. Language spoken in southern Mesopotamia — 3. ____________
4. Language related to Hebrew — 4. ____________
5. Protected the city-state from enemies and unfriendly nomads — 5. ____________
6. Of extreme importance to the Sumerians, as shown by the size and magnificence of their temples — 6. ____________
7. Sumerian society was divided into specific groups such as these; also appeared in later civilizations — 7. ____________
8. Conqueror of all city-states in Mesopotamia — 8. ____________

Directions: Use the information from Lesson 2 to complete each sentence. You may use your textbook.

9. Mesopotamians believed that ____________________, which were the largest and most impressive temples, linked the heavens and Earth.

10. The Sumerians believed in ____________________, which meant that the right to rule was god-given.

11. The empire of Akkadian ruler Sargon was said to stretch from "the sunrise to the sunset," meaning that he ruled ____________________.

12. Ur's control over Mesopotamia ended around 2000 B.C. when the city-state fell to invaders from ____________________.

Notes for Home: Your child learned about city-states in Mesopotamia.
Home Activity: Have your child find Mesopotamia on a historical map, and then draw or trace this region on a sheet of paper. Have him or her label the northern part of the region *Akkad* and the southern part *Sumer*. Ask your child to identify which countries now control these areas.

Name ______________________ Date __________ **Lesson Review**

Use with Pages 48–53.

Lesson 3: Babylonia and Assyria

Directions: Circle the term that best answers each clue.

1. King of Babylon in 1792 B.C.
   - **a.** Ashurbanipal
   - **b.** Hammurabi
2. The Babylonian Empire in 1754 B.C.
   - **a.** all of Mesopotamia
   - **b.** northern Mesopotamia
3. The Code of Hammurabi
   - **a.** code of laws for Assyrian conquerors
   - **b.** code of laws for Babylonian society
4. Assyrian homeland
   - **a.** northern Mesopotamia
   - **b.** southern Mesopotamia
5. Assyrian culture was greatly influenced by
   - **a.** Sumerian culture
   - **b.** Babylonian culture
6. Assyrians placed a high value on
   - **a.** war and conquest
   - **b.** fair laws
7. Assyrian king during the height of the Assyrian Empire
   - **a.** Ashurbanipal
   - **b.** Hammurabi
8. Location of library containing Sumerian, Akkadian, and Babylonian writings
   - **a.** Babylon
   - **b.** Nineveh

Directions: Answer the following questions on the lines provided. You may use your textbook.

9. Who was Nebuchadnezzar and what did he do? ______________________

____

____

10. What is an example of Babylonian advancement in mathematics? ______________________

____

____

11. Who conquered the Babylonian Empire in 539 B.C.? ______________________

Notes for Home: Your child learned about the Babylonians and the Assyrians.
Home Activity: Ask your child to create a campaign poster for each of the different rulers of Mesopotamia. Encourage your child to include each ruler's accomplishments in the poster.

Name ______________________ Date ____________ **Lesson Review**

Use with Pages 54–59.

Lesson 4: Hebrews, Phoenicians, and Lydians

Directions: Match each name or term to its description. Write the number of each name or term on the line provided. You may use your textbook.

1. Abraham	_____	**a.**	inventors of the first coins
2. Hebrews	_____	**b.**	chosen by God to lead the Hebrews out of Egypt
3. Canaan	_____	**c.**	new kingdom founded by King David
4. Moses	_____	**d.**	the split kingdom of Israel
5. Ten Commandments	_____	**e.**	where God sent Abraham
6. Torah	_____	**f.**	first five books of the Hebrew Bible
7. Israel	_____	**g.**	founder of Judaism
8. Israel and Judah	_____	**h.**	Abraham's people
9. Carthage	_____	**i.**	the Phoenicians' most important trading post
10. Lydians	_____	**j.**	set of laws given to Moses by God

Directions: Answer the following questions on the lines provided.

11. Why do you think Solomon was considered to be a wise ruler?

____

____

12. How did the Phoenicians link many parts of the ancient world?

____

____

13. How are the Phoenician alphabet and cuneiform writing different?

____

____

____

Notes for Home: Your child learned about the Hebrews, Phoenicians, and Lydians.
Home Activity: With your child, study U.S. coins and find the words *United States of America* on each. Ask your child to explain why he or she thinks different countries produce different coins. Discuss how daily life might be different if people still had to barter for all their goods and services.

Name ____________________ Date ____________

Thinking Skills

Use with Pages 60–61.

Make Inferences

Inferences are logical guesses that people make to explain something when all the facts are not available. The following passage was written by a young woman. It is a diary entry about a special gift.

Directions: Read the passage and make an inference about where David is. Write the answer to each question on the lines provided.

Even as a young man
my brother David dreamed of
traveling to far-off foreign lands.

Today I received a gift
from Africa. I will treasure this
gift with all my heart because I
do not know when I'll see my
brother again.

1. Who gave the gift from Africa?

____

2. How does the author feel about the gift from her brother?

____

3. How do you feel when you receive a gift from someone special?

____

____

4. What inference can you make about where David is?

____

5. Suppose you later found out that David had bartered in your hometown for the African gift. Would you change your inference? Why or why not?

____

____

____

Notes for Home: Your child learned about making inferences.
Home Activity: With your child, look through a book or magazine and examine different photos of people or animals. Without reading captions or accompanying text, ask your child to infer what is happening in each photo. Then read the surrounding information. How accurate were his or her inferences?

Name ______________________ Date __________ **Vocabulary Review**

Use with Chapter 2.

Vocabulary Review

Directions: Match each term to its description. Write the number of each term on the line provided. Not all terms will be used.

1. civilization
2. fertile
3. plain
4. plateau
5. irrigation
6. city-state
7. region
8. artisan
9. ziggurat
10. society
11. polytheism
12. scribe
13. cuneiform
14. conquer
15. empire
16. dynasty
17. conquest
18. covenant
19. monotheism
20. slavery
21. descendant
22. barter

_____ **a.** wedge-shaped writing formed in wet clay

_____ **b.** method of watering crops

_____ **c.** an area of flat land

_____ **d.** formed by establishing rules and traditions in an organized community

_____ **e.** a person who is born later to the same family

_____ **f.** the worship of one god

_____ **g.** a craftsperson, such as a potter or a weaver

_____ **h.** group of people in a complex, organized society

_____ **i.** the practice of one person owning another person

_____ **j.** a professional writer

_____ **k.** an area of high, flat land

_____ **l.** an agreement

_____ **m.** rich, good for growing

_____ **n.** a city that is an individual unit, complete with its own form of government and traditions

_____ **o.** a huge pyramid-shaped structure formed from a series of stacked rectangular platforms

_____ **p.** large territory of many places all under one ruler

_____ **q.** the worship of many gods

_____ **r.** an area with common physical features

_____ **s.** the ruling family of an empire

_____ **t.** the exchange of goods and services

Notes for Home: Your child learned about the Fertile Crescent and the civilizations that lived there.
Home Activity: With your child, write a paragraph or two using all the vocabulary words.

Name ______________________ Date __________

UNIT
1 Project Future World

Use with Page 68.

Directions: In a group, complete the chart with information to help you plan a script for a documentary about life today for people living a hundred years from now.

Object	**Description** (how people today use it)	**Clues** (what people in the future might learn from it)

Checklist for Students

_____ We chose everyday objects to include in our documentary.
_____ We wrote a description and clues about each object.
_____ We wrote a script for our documentary.
_____ We presented our documentary to the class.

Notes for Home: Your child learned how to write a documentary representing life today.
Home Activity: With your child, look for different objects in and around your home that might represent life today. Discuss what people living a hundred years from now might learn about life today from these objects.

Name ______________________ Date ____________ **Reading Social Studies**

Use with Pages 74–75.

Summarize

Directions: Read the paragraphs below and answer the questions that follow. Fill in the circle next to the right answer. You may use your textbook.

The ancient Egyptians believed strongly in life after death. Because of this belief, they built large monuments around the graves of their pharaohs, or kings. These monuments were called pyramids.

Pyramids were important to everyone in the kingdom. Egyptians believed their eternal life depended on the afterlife of their pharaoh. In turn, the quality of the pharaoh's afterlife depended largely on the superiority of his pyramid.

The pyramid for each pharaoh was built during his lifetime. The names of the groups who built the structure were written in hieroglyphs on the walls of the pyramid. The hieroglyphs also told about the life of each king.

Inside the pyramid, many treasures were stored for the pharaoh. Furniture also was placed in the tomb so that he could be near familiar things. These items were believed to make the afterlife more comfortable for the pharaoh.

1. Which of the following best summarizes the passage?

Ⓐ Hieroglyphs are the form of writing Egyptians used to preserve history.
Ⓑ Furniture was used as a symbol of wealth in ancient Egypt.
Ⓒ When they died, Egyptian pharaohs were placed in pyramids filled with riches.
Ⓓ Pharaohs were not important in Egypt.

2. The main idea of the last paragraph is:

Ⓐ Items to help a pharaoh in the afterlife were put inside the pyramid.
Ⓑ Pharaohs needed many things to enter the afterlife.
Ⓒ Egyptians built a pyramid during the life of each pharaoh.
Ⓓ Looting of the pyramids was a big problem.

Notes for Home: Your child learned how to summarize written passages.
Home Activity: Read an interesting article from a newspaper or magazine aloud to your child. Then ask him or her to verbally summarize what you read. Encourage your child to think about the "big picture."

Name ________________________ Date __________ **Vocabulary Preview**

Use with Chapter 3.

Vocabulary Preview

Directions: Match each word on the left with its definition on the right. Write the letter of the definition on the line beside each word. You may use your textbook.

___ **1.** delta	**a.** waterfall
___ **2.** silt	**b.** to unite
___ **3.** papyrus	**c.** form of writing based on pictures
___ **4.** cataract	**d.** free
___ **5.** unify	**e.** title given to a king meaning "great house"
___ **6.** pharaoh	**f.** a mixture of soil and small rocks
___ **7.** hieroglyphics	**g.** preserved Egyptian body
___ **8.** pyramid	**h.** the way people use and manage resources
___ **9.** mummy	**i.** a triangular-shaped area of soil at the mouth of a river that looks like fingers
___ **10.** economy	**j.** valuable crop used to make paper
___ **11.** independent	**k.** stone building that housed the dead

Directions: Choose three of the vocabulary words from this chapter and include them in an original sentence. Write your sentence on the lines below.

____

____

____

____

Notes for Home: Your child learned the vocabulary terms for Chapter 3.
Home Activity: Make your own hieroglyphics. Help your child make up a hieroglyphic to represent each vocabulary word. Encourage him or her to base each drawing on the meaning of the specific word.

Name ______________________ Date __________

Lesson Review

Use with Pages 78–81.

Lesson 1: The Lifeline of the Nile

Directions: Complete the following questions and statements about the Nile River. You may use your textbook.

1. Why was the Nile so important to the ancient Egyptians?

____

____

2. The dry desert land not far from the banks of the Nile is called

____.

3. Egyptians used papyrus stems to make

____.

4. What made it difficult for the ancient Egyptians to transport goods southward down the Nile?

____

____

5. What often happened when heavy rains caused the Nile to overflow?

____

6. How did the Egyptians prepare for times when the Nile did not flood enough and crops could not grow?

____

7. What technology did the Egyptians use to move water from the Nile to their crops?

____

8. The Egyptians' main god, ________________, was represented by the sun.

9. Why did the Egyptians put together a calendar?

____

Notes for Home: Your child learned how important the Nile River was to the ancient Egyptians.
Home Activity: With your child, examine how the dates are arranged in a calendar. Then have your child find the months when the Egyptians predicted the Nile would flood. Ask what season those months correspond with in the Northern Hemisphere.

Name ______________________ Date ____________ **Map and Globe Skills**

Use with Pages 82–83.

Compare Maps at Different Scales

Directions: Look at the maps of Egypt below. Then use complete sentences to answer the questions that follow. You may use your textbook.

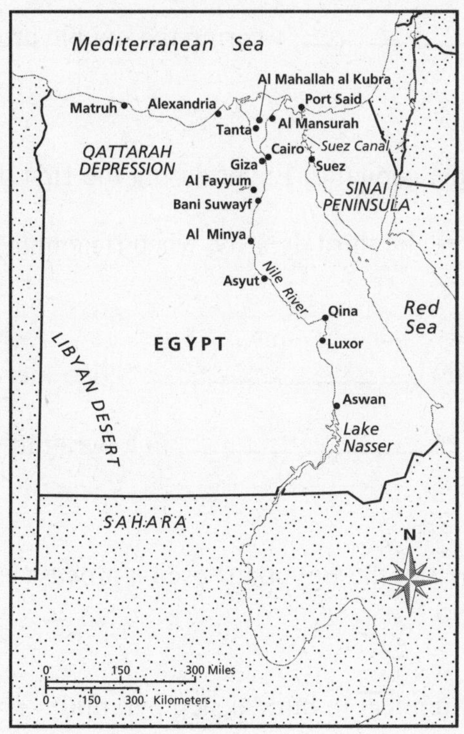

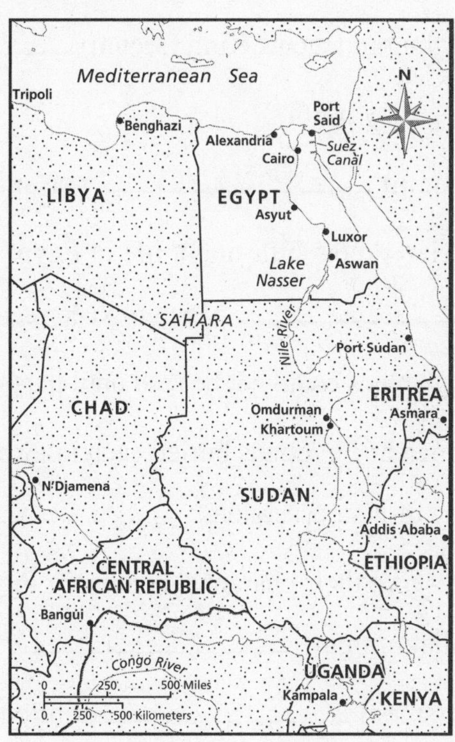

1. When might the large-scale map be most useful? ______________________________

____

____

2. When might the small-scale map be most useful? ______________________________

____

____

3. Using the map scale, about how many miles is it from Cairo, Egypt, to N'Djamena, Chad?

   Which map did you use? Why? ____

____

____

Notes for Home: Your child learned how to read maps with different scales.
Home Activity: Pretend you are planning a trip with your child beginning in Egypt. Pick various spots in Egypt and then end in Chad or Sudan. Ask your child to calculate how many miles you would travel.

Name ______________________ Date ____________ **Lesson Review**

Use with Pages 84–90.

Lesson 2: Life in Egypt

Directions: Unscramble the words below to make each sentence true. You may use your textbook.

1. According to legend, King (seenm) ________________, wearing the double crown, led his army north.
2. (sheimmp) ________________ was made the capital of Egypt during the first dynasty.
3. Historians know little about life in Egypt before the third dynasty, when (teaonhm) ________________ began to keep records.
4. Hieroglyphics could not be read until the (storate) ________________ Stone was decoded.
5. The ancient Egyptians buried each (ahorpah) ________________ in a pyramid with a variety of his possessions.
6. To preserve their pharaohs' bodies for the afterlife, the Egyptians used a process called (oumiiatmmfcin) ________________.
7. King (sreoz) ________________ hired an architect to build a step pyramid.
8. The (targe dipayrm) ________________ was the tallest human-made structure in the world until the 1800s.
9. A new middle class of artisans and scribes emerged during the (dlmedi gmondki) ____________________________.
10. The Hyksos of western Asia brought new technology to Egypt, including the (traihoc) ________________.
11. Sobeknefru and Hatshepsut were powerful (mnowe) ________________ rulers in Egypt.

Notes for Home: Your child learned about the traditions and daily lives of the ancient Egyptians.
Home Activity: Have your child draw the social pyramid of the Middle Kingdom. Discuss with him or her differences between that social pyramid and the social structure of our society today.

Name ______________________ Date __________ **Lesson Review**

Use with Pages 92–95.

Lesson 3: Nubia and Egypt

Directions: Write *T* (True) or *F* (False) on the line beside each statement. On the lines provided, rewrite each false statement to make it true. You may use your textbook.

____ **1.** Nubia was a kingdom to the south of Egypt.

____

____ **2.** Meroitic was the Nubian written language.

____

____ **3.** Just like hieroglyphics, Meroitic was translated using the Rosetta Stone.

____

____ **4.** The Nubians worshipped only one god.

____

____ **5.** The Nubians invaded Egypt in search of resources.

____

____ **6.** Egypt cut blocks of granite from Nubia's northern cliffs.

____

____ **7.** Egypt built trading centers and forts in Nubia.

____

____ **8.** Nubia expanded its borders into northern Egypt during the 1800s B.C.

____

____ **9.** Kush became free under the rule of the Hyksos.

____

____ **10.** After the 1400s B.C., Egypt became so weak that Kush won its independence.

____

____ **11.** Meroë became a great trade center in A.D. 350.

____

Notes for Home: Your child learned about the relationship between Nubia and Egypt.
Home Activity: Quiz your child about Nubia and Egypt by reading key sentences from the book with important words left out. Ask your child to supply the missing words or ideas.

Name ______________________ Date __________

Vocabulary Review

Use with Chapter 3.

Vocabulary Review

Directions: Use the vocabulary words from Chapter 3 to complete the crossword puzzle.

Across

1. mixture of soil and small rocks
3. looks like spread-out fingers
4. "great house"
7. house for the dead
8. waterfall
9. a preserved Egyptian body
11. unite

Down

2. free
5. "sacred carvings"
6. the way people use and manage resources
10. used to make paper

Notes for Home: Your child learned the vocabulary words for Chapter 3.
Home Activity: With your child, make two sets of vocabulary cards. On one set, write all 11 vocabulary words. On the other set, write the definitions. Shuffle the cards and place them all face down. Then take turns looking for matches.

Name ______________________ Date ____________ **Vocabulary Preview**

Use with Chapter 4.

Vocabulary Preview

Directions: Circle the word that best completes each sentence. Then write the definition of that word in the space provided. You may use your textbook.

1. The fertile land on the plain is enriched by (double cropping, loess).

____

2. Crops in the North China Plain often are grown using a broad (terrace, pictograph).

____

3. A kind of wall known as a (levee, terrace) helps contain the Huang River.

____

4. Rice and sugar cane often are used for (oracle bones, double cropping).

____

5. The Chinese language is written using a type of symbol called a (loess, pictograph).

____

6. An (ancestor, oracle bone) was a tool used to tell the future.

____

7. Qin was divided into 36 (provinces, terraces).

____

8. The first Han ruler was Han Gaozu, whose name means "High (Nobility, Ancestor)."

____

9. Wu Di made people take (civil service, middleman) exams to work for the government.

____

10. A new way to trade during the Han dynasty involved (double cropping, a middleman).

____

11. Confucius could become a scholar because of his (nobility, oracle bone).

____

Notes for Home: Your child learned the vocabulary words for Chapter 4.
Home Activity: With your child, take turns illustrating the different vocabulary words. Have the person who is not drawing guess which word is being illustrated. Discuss the definitions as you go.

Name ______________________ Date ____________ **Lesson Review**

Use with Pages 100–103.

Lesson 1: The Geography of China

Directions: Choose the term from the box below that best completes each sentence. Not all of the terms will be used.

Asia	Guangxi Zhungzu	North China Plain
Beijing	Gulf of Tonkin	Tibetan Plateau
contrasts	Himalayas	the world
Europe	Huang River	yellow
Gobi	loess	Zhuang
4,300	Vietnamese	3,400

1. China is the largest country in ______________.
2. Due to its great size, China is a land of ______________.
3. A large portion of China's food comes from the ______________.
4. ______________ is the country's capital and has been a center of culture and government since the 1200s.
5. The Huang River is almost ______________ miles long from start to finish.
6. The ______________ stretches across parts of Mongolia and China.
7. Dissolved silt makes the ______________ look yellow.
8. The Guangxi Zhungzu is bordered on the south by the ______________.
9. Farming and fishing are very important to the people in the ______________ region.
10. The largest minority group in China is the ______________.
11. The ______________ is known as the Roof of the World.
12. The ______________ actually are located in more than one country.

Notes for Home: Your child learned about the geography of China.
Home Activity: Ask your child to make a list of things he or she might take on a nature tour of China. Discuss why each item would be beneficial and where it might be used.

Name ______________________ Date ____________ **Chart and Graph Skills**

Use with Pages 104–105.

Interpret Climographs

Directions: Use the graph below to answer the questions that follow. You may use your textbook.

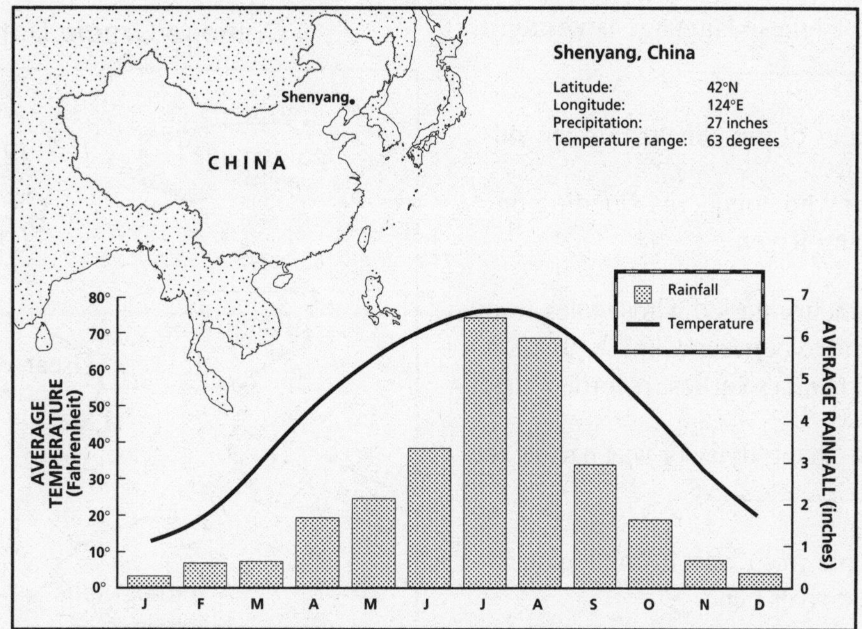

1. What does this climograph show? ______________________

____

2. Which two months show the most rainfall? ______________________

____

3. About how many inches of rain does Shenyang receive in September? ______________________

____

4. What is the average temperature during the month of May? ______________________

5. In what month does the least amount of rain fall? ______________________

Notes for Home: Your child learned how to use a climograph.
Home Activity: Have your child go to **www.worldclimate.com** to find the weather statistics for your city or area. Then help your child make his or her own climograph.

Name ______________________ Date ___________

Lesson Review

Use with Pages 106–112.

Lesson 2: China's Past

Directions: Match each phrase with the oracle bone it describes. Write the letter of the correct oracle bone on the line beside each phrase. You may use your textbook.

____ **1.** The Chinese language is written in __________.

____ **2.** creator of the universe, in legends

____ **3.** hero who conquered flooding on Huang River

____ **4.** legendary period whose tales formed a bridge between China's prehistory and China's earliest recorded history

____ **5.** The Shang dynasty was part of the __________ Age.

____ **6.** people from west of the Huang's great river bend

____ **7.** Women were in charge of producing __________.

____ **8.** second part of the Zhou dynasty

____ **9.** state divided into 36 provinces

____ **10.** built to protect the empire from northern invaders

____ **11.** first Han ruler

____ **12.** built new roads to improve transportation

____ **13.** wrote the first complete history of China

____ **14.** the only land connection between China and the rest of the world

Chinese Oracle Bones

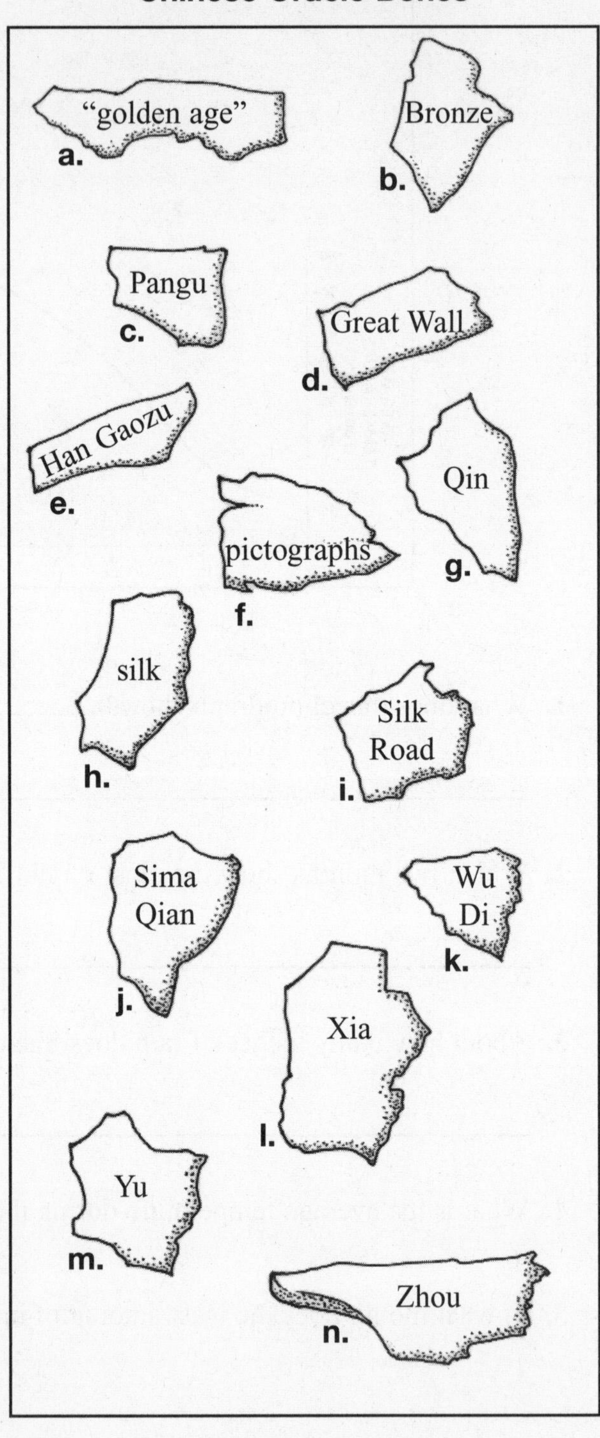

Notes for Home: Your child learned about China's past.
Home Activity: With your child, use the textbook to practice pronouncing the names from this lesson. Discuss the different sounds assigned to letters such as *x* and *q*.

Name ______________________ Date __________ **Lesson Review**

Use with Pages 114–117.

Lesson 3: Legacy of Thought

Directions: The underlined terms below have been scrambled so that each appears in the wrong sentence. Write each term on the line beside the sentence where it actually belongs. You may use your textbook.

______________ **1.** The Great Temple houses a statue of respect.

______________ **2.** Confucius was sometimes called Mencius, or Kung Fuzi.

______________ **3.** Confucius could be educated as a scholar because his family was of some morals.

______________ **4.** Master Kung traveled with a group of schools.

______________ **5.** Confucius was a teacher of Laozi.

______________ **6.** Disciples are at the core of Confucianism.

______________ **7.** Confucius taught that finding the authority helped people make balanced decisions.

______________ **8.** In Confucianism a ruler was seen as a great nobility.

______________ **9.** According to Confucius, the people needed to have harmony for their ruler.

______________ **10.** Confucius lived in the period called the "hundred virtues of thought."

______________ **11.** Master Kung was a follower of Confucius who believed that people were good by nature.

______________ **12.** The first great teacher of Daoism was Confucius.

______________ **13.** Daoists believe that people should live in middle way with nature.

Notes for Home: Your child learned about the basics of Confucianism and Daoism.
Home Activity: With your child, create a chart to compare and contrast Confucianism and Daoism. List and discuss the background and basic concepts of each way of thinking.

Name ______________________ Date ____________ **Vocabulary Review**

Use with Chapter 4.

Vocabulary Review

Directions: Use each of the following vocabulary words in an original sentence. Write your sentences on the lines provided. You may use the plural form of a word, if necessary.

1. loess ______________________
2. terrace ______________________
3. levee ______________________
4. double cropping ______________________
5. pictograph ______________________
6. oracle bone ______________________
7. province ______________________
8. ancestor ______________________
9. civil service ______________________
10. middleman ______________________
11. nobility ______________________

Notes for Home: Your child learned the vocabulary words for Chapter 4.
Home Activity: Use the vocabulary words above in a game with your child. Write each word on a card and shuffle all the cards. Then have one person supply one-word clues until the other person guesses each word.

Name ________________________ Date __________

Vocabulary Preview

Directions: Use the vocabulary words from Chapter 5 to complete the crossword puzzle. You may use your textbook.

Across

3. lifelong social group
6. process through which a person is believed to go from one life to the next
7. serf
8. _______ season (rainy season)
9. state of pure goodness

Down

1. Living on the food you grow is called _______ farming.
2. large region separated by water from other land areas
4. a way of clearing the mind
5. priest or teacher

Notes for Home: Your child learned the vocabulary words for Chapter 5.
Home Activity: Have your child write a sentence for each vocabulary word. Then work together to use these sentences to make up a story.

Name ______________________ Date ____________ **Lesson Review**

Use with Pages 122–127.

Lesson 1: Geography of South Asia

Directions: Label the map by writing the number of each place listed below on the map where it is located. You may use your textbook or a map of South Asia.

1. Himalayas
2. Mount Everest
3. India
4. Pakistan
5. Nepal
6. Bhutan
7. Afghanistan
8. Bangladesh
9. Sri Lanka
10. Maldive Islands
11. Hindu Kush
12. Indian Ocean
13. Indo-Ganges Plain
14. Deccan Plateau
15. Eastern Ghats
16. Western Ghats

South Asia

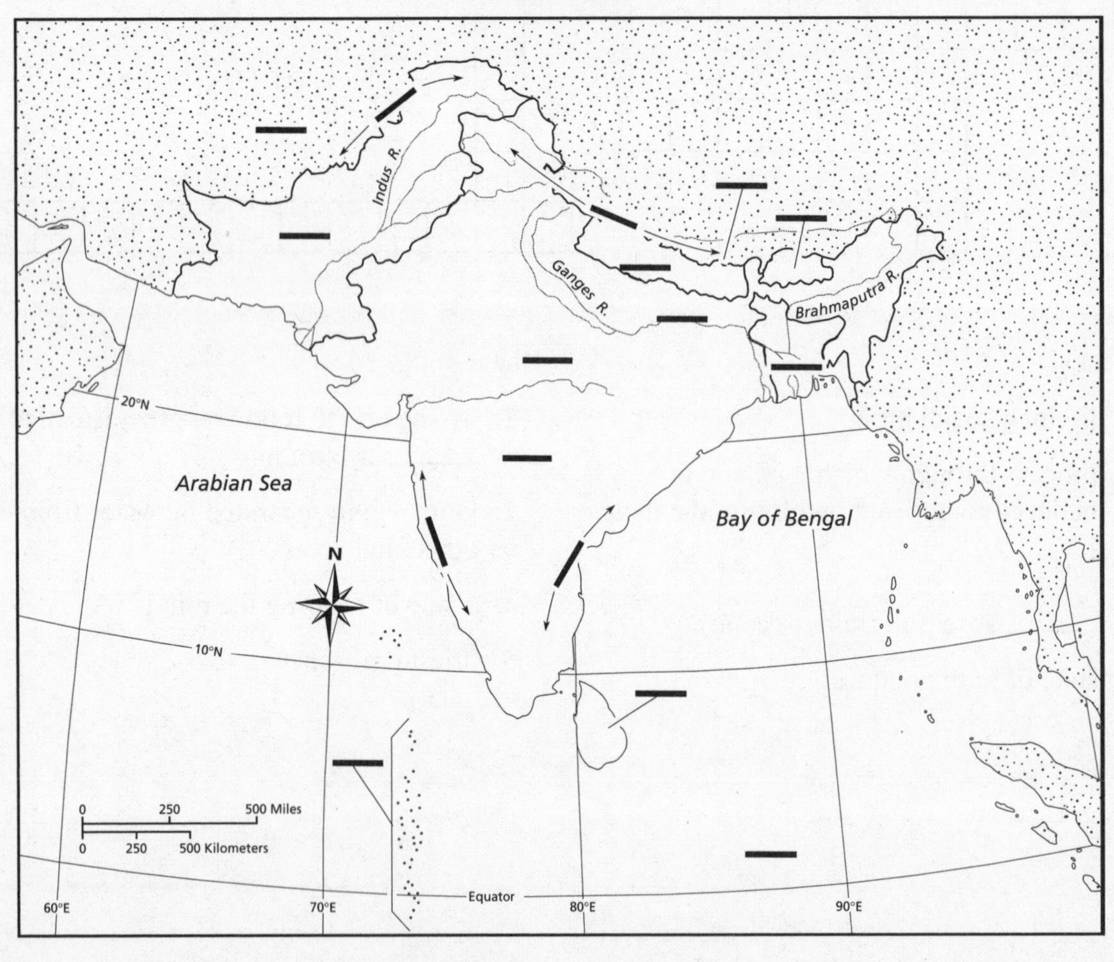

Notes for Home: Your child learned about the geography of South Asia.
Home Activity: With your child, use the map and information in the lesson to compare and contrast the geography of South Asia with the geography of the United States.

Name ______________________ Date ____________ **Lesson Review**

Use with Pages 128–134.

Lesson 2: India and Persia

Directions: Read each of the following descriptions and decide if it is related to the Aryan Empire (*A*), Persian Empire (*P*), Mauryan Empire (*M*), or Gupta Empire (*G*). Write the appropriate letter on the line beside each description. You may use your textbook.

____ **1.** Developed the number system we use today

____ **2.** Founded the religion of Zoroastrianism

____ **3.** Developed roads and trade in India

____ **4.** Lasted from about 320 B.C. to about 185 B.C.

____ **5.** Designed stone temples

____ **6.** Lasted from about 1500 B.C. to about 550 B.C.

____ **7.** First Indian empire

____ **8.** Lasted from about 550 B.C. to about 320 B.C.

____ **9.** Had civil service workers, a powerful army, and an army of spies

____ **10.** Nomads who crossed the Hindu Kush

____ **11.** Used stone columns to mark territory and to make announcements

____ **12.** Lasted from about A.D. 320 to about A.D. 520

____ **13.** Sanskrit became the language of the wealthy

____ **14.** Recorded their stories and songs in the Vedas, or "Books of Knowledge"

____ **15.** Groups were headed by a rajah

____ **16.** Founder was Cyrus II

Notes for Home: Your child learned characteristics of the different empires in India and Persia.
Home Activity: Discuss with your child the contributions of each empire. Then work together to create a time line of all the empires.

Name ______________________ Date __________ **Lesson Review**

Use with Pages 136–139.

Lesson 3: Hinduism

Directions: To fill out the tree chart below, write one Hindu belief on each of the six branches. Then write the origin of the Hindu religion on the line at the base of the tree. You may use your textbook.

Notes for Home: Your child learned about the origin and some beliefs of the Hindu religion.
Home Activity: With your child, create a chart to compare and contrast Hinduism and other religions with which he or she is familiar.

Name ______________________ Date __________ **Lesson Review**

Use with Pages 140–143.

Lesson 4: Buddhism

Directions: Number the following events in Siddhartha Gautama's life in order from *1* (earliest) to *10* (most recent). Then fill in the blanks to complete the Four Noble Truths of Buddhism. You may use your textbook.

___ **1.** Siddhartha sits under a tree and meditates.

___ **2.** He becomes enlightened.

___ **3.** After feeling very weak, he leaves the group.

___ **4.** He travels and teaches for nearly 50 years.

___ **5.** In a village, Siddhartha sees a very sick person.

___ **6.** He joins a group of men who sought understanding and simple living.

___ **7.** Siddhartha is kept inside the palace.

___ **8.** He sees a morning star.

___ **9.** After becoming an adult, he leaves the palace.

___ **10.** Siddhartha fasts for six years.

The Four Noble Truths of Buddhism:

1. ______________ is part of life for all people.

2. People suffer because they ______________ so many things in life.

3. If people can ______________ themselves from wanting so many things, they will not suffer.

4. People can free themselves from wants and from suffering by following the ______________.

Notes for Home: Your child learned about the origins and beliefs of Buddhism.
Home Activity: Discuss the Four Noble Truths with your child. Then have him or her explain the difference between wants and needs. Together, brainstorm a list of each.

Name ______________________ Date __________

Use with Pages 144–145.

Gather and Report Information

Directions: Imagine you are writing a research paper about eastern religions or the Mauryan Empire. Answer the questions below. You may use your textbook.

1. What might be your hypothesis? ______________________

____

2. Where would you look for information? ______________________

____

3. List three terms that you might look up to help research your topic. ______________________

____

____

4. Why should you evaluate your sources? ______________________

____

5. What should you include in each paragraph? Why? ______________________

____

6. In what order should your sources be listed in a bibliography? ______________________

____

Notes for Home: Your child learned how to research and write a report.
Home Activity: Have your child choose a subject in which he or she is interested. Then provide pointers on how to effectively research the topic on the Internet or at the library.

Name ______________________ Date __________ **Vocabulary Review**

Use with Chapter 5.

Vocabulary Review

Directions: Fill in the spaces below with the vocabulary word that best completes each sentence. Then unscramble the letters marked with a star to discover the mystery phrase related to Chapter 5. You may use your textbook.

1. South Asia is called a _ _ _ _ _ _ _ _ _ _* _ _ _ _ _ because it is a large region separated by water from other land areas.
2. The _ _ _* _ _ _ _ _ _ _* _ _ _ _ _ in South Asia lasts from June through September.
3. Many families from South Asia practice _ _ _ _ _ _ _ _ _ _ _ _* _ _ _ _ _ _ _* _ _. They do not produce extra crops to sell.
4. In the Aryan culture, a _ _ _* _ _ _ _ _ held the highest position in society.
5. An Aryan _ _ _* _ _ was ordered to farm the land and serve others.
6. Hindus believe in _ _ _ _ _ _ _ _ _ _ _ _* _ _ _ _, a process in which a person is reborn into a new life.
7. In India every Hindu is a member of a _* _ _ _ _.
8. Siddhartha spent several years fasting and practicing _ _ _ _ _ _ _* _ _ _ _.
9. Buddha believed that all people could achieve _ _ _ _* _ _ _ _ _ _ _ _ _ _* _.

Mystery Phrase: _ _ _ _ _ _ _ _ _ _ _ _ _ _ _ and Persia

Notes for Home: Your child learned the vocabulary words for Chapter 5.
Home Activity: With your child, write each vocabulary word on the front of a separate index card. Write the definition of each word on the back. Show your child one side of the card and have him or her answer with the hidden word or definition.

Name ______________________ Date __________

Discovery Channel School

Unit 2 Project All About a Pyramid

Use with Page 152.

Directions: In a group, take visitors on a video tour of an Egyptian pyramid.

1. The name of the Egyptian pyramid: ______________________.

2. Features about the pyramid included in the tour:

   ____location ____why it was built ____how it was built ____how long it took to build

   ____size and dimensions ____who is buried inside ____treasures inside

   ____the pharaoh's reign ____other features: ______________________

3. A drawing of the pyramid with important parts labeled:

Checklist for Students

_____ We chose an Egyptian pyramid for our video tour.
_____ We researched aspects of the pyramid.
_____ We made a poster or model of the pyramid.
_____ We labeled important parts of the pyramid.
_____ We presented our video tour to the class.

Notes for Home: Your child learned about Egyptian pyramids.
Home Activity: With your child, review the script for the video tour. Confirm how your child will participate in the presentation and make sure all important features are included in the tour.

Name ______________________ Date ______________ **Reading Social Studies**

Use with Pages 158–159.

Compare and Contrast

When you compare two items, you tell how they are alike. When you contrast them, you tell how they are different.

Directions: Read the passage. Answer the following questions.

Compare and Contrast Important Stones of Mesoamerica

Jade, basalt, and obsidian were important resources to the ancient Olmec people. They used these stones for several different purposes. Jade was carved into small figurines, ceremonial axes, and jewelry. The Olmec often traded their jade figurines for other things they wanted or needed. Usually green in color, jade was very durable and was highly prized. Both jade and basalt were used for making statues.

While jade statues were small, the basalt statues were much larger. The Olmec carved basalt into thrones and altars. However, most of the basalt was carved to form giant heads. These heads ranged from 5 to 11 feet tall. Often dark gray to black in color, basalt is a kind of volcanic rock.

Like basalt, obsidian also is a dark-colored rock formed from volcanoes. However, unlike basalt and jade, obsidian is a natural glass with sharp edges. The Olmec used it to make weapons, such as blades and dart points. All three materials—jade, basalt, and obsidian—were mined in outlying regions for use in the Olmec cultural center. The Olmec skillfully used these natural resources of Mesoamerica.

1. What is one way obsidian is different from jade and basalt?

Ⓐ Obsidian was an important resource to the Olmec.
Ⓑ Obsidian is a natural glass.
Ⓒ Obsidian was used by the Olmec for trade.
Ⓓ Obsidian has a dark color.

2. What is one way jade, basalt, and obsidian are similar?

Ⓐ They all are from Guatemala.
Ⓑ They all are bright green in color.
Ⓒ The Olmec used them all for making statues.
Ⓓ They all are natural resources.

Notes for Home: Your child learned how to compare and contrast.
Home Activity: With your child, compare and contrast life today and life in early American civilizations.

Name ______________________ Date ____________ **Vocabulary Preview**

Use with Chapter 6.

Vocabulary Preview

Directions: Use the vocabulary words from Chapter 6 to complete the crossword puzzle. You may use your textbook.

Across

1. folding-screen book
4. arm of land sticking into the sea
6. hired soldier
7. sink hole that was sacred to the Maya as a source of water
8. agreement to work with other city-states

Down

1. island built by the Mexica
2. form of government in which the leader and the ruling classes are believed to represent the will of the gods
3. raised bridge made of land
5. structure that carries flowing water

Notes for Home: Your child learned the vocabulary terms for Chapter 6.
Home Activity: Have your child use each term in an original sentence that reflects his or her understanding of the meaning of the terms.

Name ______________________ Date __________ **Lesson Review**

Use with Pages 162–165.

Lesson 1: Geography of Mesoamerica

Directions: Answer the following questions on the lines provided. You may use your textbook.

1. What did the people of Mesoamerica do with jade, basalt, and obsidian?

____

____

____

2. What were the two main mountain ranges in northern Mesoamerica?

____

3. Describe the climate of Mesoamerica.

____

____

4. What is the land like along the Gulf of Mexico?

____

____

5. When it rains, what happens to the limestone of the Yucatán Peninsula?

____

____

6. What are sink holes? What do they provide?

____

7. What did the cultures of the peoples of Mesoamerica have in common?

____

____

8. Describe a Mesoamerican city.

____

____

Notes for Home: Your child learned about the geography and the people of Mesoamerica.
Home Activity: Discuss with your child what it might have been like to live in Mesoamerica. Ask him or her whether he or she would rather have lived in the mountains or along the coast and why.

Name ______________________ Date ____________ **Map and Globe Skills**

Use with Pages 166–167.

Use Map Projections

Directions: Answer the questions about map projections in the space provided.

1. What are map projections?

____

____

____

2. What would you have to do to the surface of a round object, such as a grapefruit, if you wanted it to lie flat?

____

____

3. What characteristics of Earth's surface are distorted by different map projections?

____

____

Directions: Decide whether each statement below describes an Equal-area, Robinson, or Mercator map. For Equal-area write *E* in the blank, for Robinson write *R*, and for Mercator write *M*. You may use your textbook.

____ **4.** often used for maps of the United States

____ **5.** true only at the center point

____ **6.** distortion increases toward the poles

____ **7.** distortion increases away from a line between the equator and a pole

____ **8.** true at the equator

____ **9.** true along a line between the equator and a pole

____ **10.** often used for comparing the size (but not the shape) of land masses

____ **11.** distortion is worst at the edge of the map

____ **12.** often used for navigation charts

Notes for Home: Your child learned about map projections.
Home Activity: With your child, find a map. Discuss which type of map projection was used, which features are most distorted, where the distortions occur, and where the map is the most true.

Name ______________________ Date ____________ **Lesson Review**

Use with Pages 168–173.

Lesson 2: The Olmec and the Maya

The Olmec and Mayan civilizations were both similar and different.

Directions: In the blank beside each description, write an *O* if the phrase describes the Olmec, an *M* if it describes the Maya, or a *B* if it describes both the Olmec and the Maya.

____ **1.** government was a theocracy

____ **2.** also called the "Mother Culture"

____ **3.** raised corn, beans, and squash

____ **4.** were skilled mathematicians

____ **5.** believed cenotes were a way to communicate with the gods

____ **6.** developed a calendar

____ **7.** constructed giant stone heads

____ **8.** built more than 3,000 structures in Tikal

____ **9.** lasted from about 1200 B.C. to about 300 B.C.

____ **10.** divided into social classes based on wealth and power

____ **11.** developed a system of writing

____ **12.** built observatories, palaces, plazas, baths, reservoirs, and aqueducts

____ **13.** may have disappeared as a result of invasion, crop failures, or civil war

____ **14.** may have migrated east

Notes for Home: Your child learned about the civilizations of the Olmec and the Maya.
Home Activity: With your child, discuss the developments of the Olmec and the Maya. Ask him or her how those developments may affect his or her own life today.

Name ______________________ Date ____________ **Lesson Review**

Use with Pages 174–180.

Lesson 3: The Aztecs

Directions: Match each word with its description. Write the letter of the description in the blank beside the word on the left. You may use your textbook.

____ **1.** Aztec

____ **2.** Mexica

____ **3.** mercenaries

____ **4.** Tenochtitlan

____ **5.** chinampas

____ **6.** Moctezuma I

____ **7.** Quetzalcóatl

____ **8.** human sacrifices

____ **9.** Moctezuma II

____ **10.** Hernando Cortés

a. the Spanish explorer who some Aztecs believed was Quetzalcóatl

b. a god of creation to the Aztecs

c. floating islands

d. what the early Aztecs called themselves

e. what the Aztecs believed they had to offer to honor their gods

f. the city the Aztecs built on two islands in Lake Texcoco

g. hired soldiers

h. ruled the Aztec Empire from 1440 to 1469

i. emperor during the Aztec's greatest period of power and wealth

j. the last great civilization of ancient Mesoamerica

Directions: On the lines below, describe the Aztec game of ulama.

____

____

____

____

Notes for Home: Your child learned about the Aztecs.
Home Activity: With your child, discuss the role religion had in the Aztec culture. How is it similar to and different from the various religions practiced in your community today?

Vocabulary Review

Directions: Fill in the blank with the correct word from the box below. You may use your textbook.

peninsula	aqueduct	chinampa
cenote	codex	causeway
theocracy	mercenary	alliance

1. An ____________, or an agreement to work with another city-state, would help Tenochtitlan grow.

2. The Maya sometimes got water from an ____________, or a structure that carries flowing water.

3. Olmec government was a ____________, in which the leader or ruling classes are believed to represent the will of the gods.

4. A ____________ is an arm of land sticking into the sea so that it is nearly surrounded by water.

5. A sink hole that forms a natural well was known to the Mayan people as a ____________.

6. The Mayan ____________, or folding-screen book, was written in hieroglyphics.

7. A ____________ was an island built by the Mexica to make more room.

8. A ____________ was sometimes built to connect the Mexica's artificial islands.

9. Sometimes one of the Mexica would serve as a ____________, or a hired soldier.

Notes for Home: Your child learned the vocabulary terms for Chapter 6.
Home Activity: Have your child imagine what a workday might have been like in the life of a Mesoamerican. Encourage him or her to describe this life using the vocabulary words from the chapter.

Name ______________________ Date __________

Vocabulary Preview

Use with Chapter 7.

Vocabulary Preview

Directions: Unscramble the word in parentheses to complete each sentence. You may use your textbook.

1. A group of islands is an (erpigolhcaa) ____________.
2. A rope with various lengths and colors of cords is a (uiqup) ____________.
3. A place that has a distinct climate and specific types of plants and animals is called a (meibo) ____________.
4. Much of central and southern South America is (brusc adnl) ____________, or areas of low-growing vegetation.
5. An area of very moist soil, such as a swamp, is a (dtalewn) ____________.

Directions: Write a short paragraph using four of the words you unscrambled above. Write your paragraph on the lines provided.

____

____

____

____

____

____

____

____

____

____

____

Notes for Home: Your child learned the vocabulary terms for Chapter 7.
Home Activity: With your child, write each vocabulary term on a separate index card. Then hold each card up and have your child define the word.

Name ______________________ Date ____________ **Lesson Review**

Use with Pages 186–189.

Lesson 1: Geography of South America

Directions: Imagine you are on a vacation in South America. Write a letter to one of your friends back home describing the people, places, and things you see there. Be sure to use specific names of your favorite places. You may use your textbook.

___

___

___

___

___

___

___

___

___

___

___

___

___

___

___

___

___

___

___

Notes for Home: Your child learned about the geography of South America.
Home Activity: With your child, look at a map of South America. Help him or her point out some important geographical features of this continent, such as mountains, coastlines, and rivers.

Name ______________________ Date ____________ **Lesson Review**

Use with Pages 190–193.

Lesson 2: The Chavín and the Mochica

Directions: Compare the Chavín and the Mochica by filling in the chart below. You may use your textbook.

	Chavín	Mochica
During what time period did they live?		
Where did they live?		
What did they leave behind?		
What happened to end their civilization?		
Where did their names come from?		
How did we learn about them?		

Notes for Home: Your child learned about the Chavín and the Mochica.
Home Activity: Both the Chavín and Mochica civilizations suddenly disappeared. With your child, discuss what you think might have happened to these civilizations. Ask whether he or she thinks a community could suddenly disappear today? Why or why not?

Name ______________________ Date __________

Use with Pages 194–195.

Use Latitude and Longitude

Directions: Use the map below to help you answer the questions. If you cannot tell the exact answer from the map, use your best estimate.

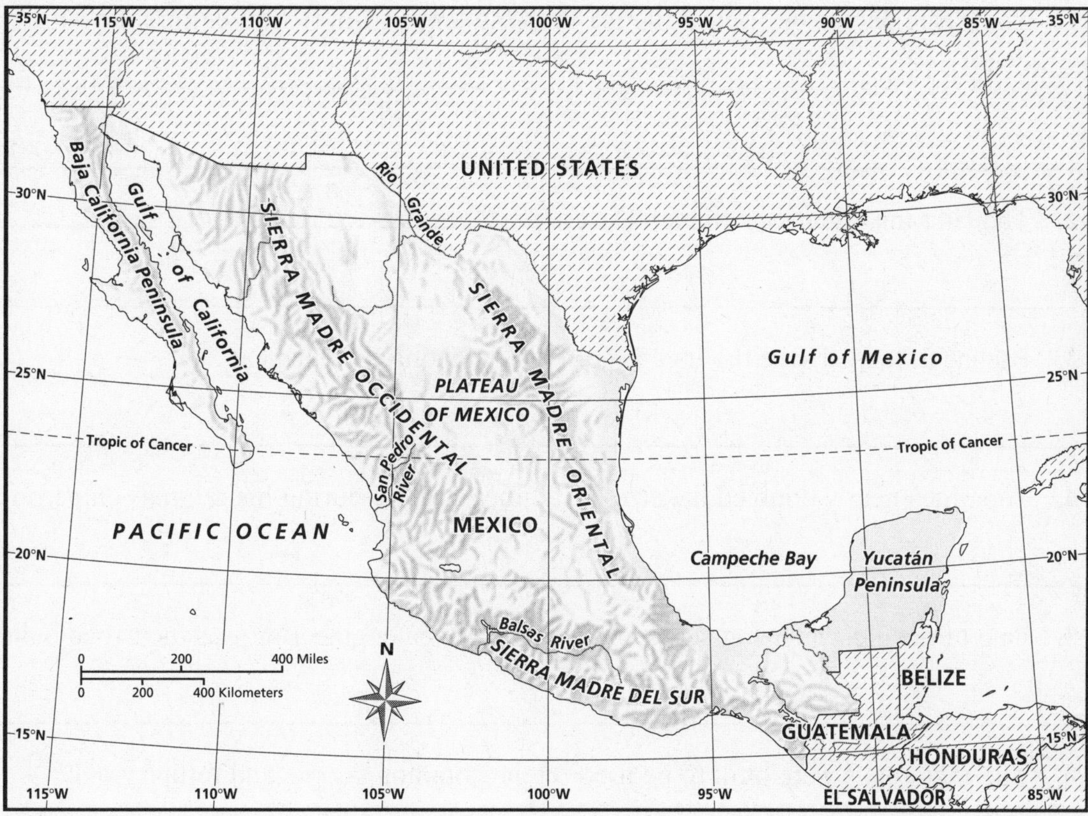

1. Between which two lines of longitude can the Plateau of Mexico be found?

____

2. Between which two lines of latitude can the Baja California Peninsula be found?

____

3. Between which two lines of latitude and two lines of longitude is the Sierra Madre Oriental mountain range found?

____

4. Between which two lines of latitude and two lines of longitude is the Sierra Madre Occidental mountain range found?

____

Notes for Home: Your child learned how to use latitude and longitude on a map.
Home Activity: With your child, pick several places of interest. Try to find the latitude and longitude of these places using maps and/or the Internet.

Name ______________________ Date __________ **Lesson Review**

Use with Pages 196–201.

Lesson 3: The Inca

Directions: Write *T* (True) or *F* (False) on the line beside each sentence. If the sentence is false, rewrite the false part to make it true. You may use your textbook.

____ **1.** The Aztec people of South America built the largest and richest empire the Americas had ever seen. ______________________

____

____ **2.** The first Inca ruler was Manco Cuzco. ______________________

____

____ **3.** Pachacuti helped save the Inca Empire by defeating the Chancas.

____

____ **4.** Topa Inca nearly doubled the size of the Inca Empire during his reign as emperor.

____

____ **5.** One of the most amazing accomplishments of Inca engineering was their road building.

____

____ **6.** The Inca roads were built to be used by the common people and military only.

____

____ **7.** When the Incas conquered new peoples and territories, they allowed the conquered rulers to stay in power. ______________________

____

____ **8.** The Inca never developed a system of writing. ______________________

____

____ **9.** A quipu was a rope with various lengths and colors of vines.

____

____ **10.** Francisco Pizarro used horses and firearms to defeat the Inca. ______________________

____

Notes for Home: Your child learned about the Inca.
Home Activity: Ask your child what qualities make a good leader. With your child, discuss who he or she thinks was the best emperor of the Inca Empire.

Vocabulary Review

Directions: Match each vocabulary word to its meaning. Write the letter of the correct definition on the line next to each word. You may use your glossary.

____ **1.** wetland

____ **2.** biome

____ **3.** scrub land

____ **4.** archipelago

____ **5.** quipu

a. rope with various lengths and colors of cords

b. place that has a distinct climate and specific types of plants and animals

c. area of very moist soil, such as a swamp

d. area of low-growing vegetation

e. group of islands

Directions: On the lines below, write one important or interesting fact about the early peoples of South America. Use at least one of the vocabulary terms above in your description.

____

____

____

____

____

Notes for Home: Your child learned the vocabulary terms for Chapter 7.
Home Activity: With your child, play a vocabulary game. Write each term on a note card or slip of paper and turn the cards face down. Take turns selecting a card and drawing clues for that word. When the term is guessed correctly, discuss its definition.

Name ____________________ Date __________ **Vocabulary Preview**

Use with Chapter 8.

Vocabulary Preview

Directions: Circle the term in the parentheses that completes each sentence.

1. A (long house, tundra) is a cold and treeless land.
2. A (wigwam, pueblo) was built from adobe bricks.
3. The people of the Mississippian culture used a (temple mound, pit house) for religious and ceremonial purposes.
4. A (sod house, long house) is rectangular and made of logs covered by bark.
5. To make a (basin and range, pit house), you must start by digging a hole in the ground.
6. A smaller stream or river that flows into a larger river is known as a (tributary, pueblo).
7. A framework of twigs, logs, branches, or vines smeared with mud-like plaster is called a (wattle, snowhouse).
8. A temporary shelter built from blocks of soil and vegetation cut from the frozen ground is a (burial mound, sod house).
9. An important person in the Adena culture was usually buried in a (burial mound, temple mound).
10. A (basin and range, tundra) is a low area alternating with a small mountain range.
11. A temporary shelter made of blocks cut from snow is a (snowhouse, long house).
12. An (adobe, arid) climate is dry.
13. (Adobe, Wattle) brick can be stacked to form shelters.
14. A dome-shaped frame of branches covered with animal skins or woven mats is called a (wigwam, tundra).
15. If you go to the Southwest today, you might talk to a (descendant, tributary) of the Anasazi.

Notes for Home: Your child learned the vocabulary terms for Chapter 8.
Home Activity: With your child, take turns using the vocabulary terms in original sentences.

Name ______________________ Date __________ **Lesson Review**

Use with Pages 208–211.

Lesson 1: Geography of North America

Directions: Write a short description of each term on the lines provided. Then draw a small picture based on your description. You may use your textbook.

1. Rocky Mountains

____

____

____

2. Great Basin

____

____

____

3. Great Plains

____

____

____

4. Mississippi River

____

____

____

5. Canadian Shield

____

____

____

Notes for Home: Your child learned about the geography of North America.
Home Activity: With your child, pretend you are planning a trip to one of the places discussed in the lesson. Talk about what you should pack, what features you might see on the drive there, and what you might see at your destination.

Name ____________________ Date __________ **Lesson Review**

Use with Pages 212–215.

Lesson 2: The Southwestern Peoples

Directions: Complete the concept maps below. You may use your textbook.

Hohokam

Where did they live?
1.

What did they do?
3.

Houses
2.

Why did they leave?
4.

Anasazi

Where did they live?
5.

What did they do?
7.

Houses
6.

Why did they leave?
8.

Notes for Home: Your child learned about the Southwestern peoples.
Home Activity: With your child, use the graphic organizers above along with the textbook to compare and contrast the Hohokam and the Anasazi.

Name ______________________ Date ____________ **Thinking Skills**

Use with Pages 216–217.

Detect Bias

Bias is a strong opinion or set of opinions based on powerful feelings, rather than careful reasoning.

Directions: Determine if the statements below are biased. If so, state whether they are based on *generalization, lack of evidence, strong language,* or *hidden reason*. If a statement is not biased, write *not biased.*

1. The Hohokam made magnificent pit houses.

____

2. All of the Inca thought it was important to form alliances.

____

3. The officials who were closest to emperors were each responsible for about 10,000 Inca subjects. ____

4. Ancient Native Americans enjoyed swimming.

____

5. A young Hohokam boy said that it was good that the Anasazi moved away.

____

6. A peninsula is an arm of land sticking into the sea.

____

7. All of the Olmec people were farmers.

____

8. The Maya were the most amazing of all the ancient Native Americans.

____

9. The center of the Aztec Empire was Tenochtitlan and the Valley of Mexico.

____

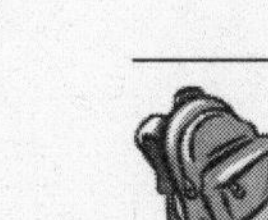

Notes for Home: Your child learned how to detect bias.
Home Activity: With your child, look through a newspaper or magazine and try to find biased statements. Discuss what the bias is based on and how and why the speaker made the specific statement.

Name ______________________ Date ____________ **Lesson Review**

Use with Pages 218–221.

Lesson 3: The Mound Builders

Directions: Use the terms in the box to complete each sentence with information from Lesson 3. Some terms will be used more than once. You may use your textbook.

Hopewell	200 years	Great Serpent Mound
Adena	burial	artifacts
Cahokia	Mississippian	specialized

1. One of the first groups of mound builders was the ______________ culture.
2. The type of mounds they built were ______________ mounds.
3. One of the most impressive Adena mounds is the ______________ ______________.
4. The ______________ lived in houses similar to wigwams.
5. Some ______________ in Hopewell mounds came from as far away as present-day Florida, Canada, and the Rocky Mountains.
6. Archaeologists believe that the Hopewell civilization was advanced enough to have ______________ artists and craftspeople.
7. No one knows what happened to the ______________ or the ______________ cultures.
8. The ______________ culture built temple mounds.
9. ______________ is the largest temple mound site.
10. In the ______________ culture, priests lived on top of some temple mounds.
11. The largest temple mound took more than ______________ to build.
12. At the ______________ Mounds State Historic Site in Illinois, you can see firsthand the wonders of the mound builders of North America.

Notes for Home: Your child learned about the mound builders of North America.
Home Activity: Discuss with your child the different types of mounds and mound builders. Ask him or her why he or she thinks different cultures built different types of mounds.

Name ______________________ Date ____________ **Lesson Review**

Use with Pages 222–224.

Lesson 4: Early Canadians

Directions: Determine whether the statements below are true or false. Circle *T* for True or *F* for False. You may use your textbook.

T F 1. North America is a land of extreme cold and few natural resources.

T F 2. The Inuit were skilled at surviving in what is today northern Canada.

T F 3. Most of what the Inuit needed came from caribou and seal.

T F 4. Seal horns sometimes were used as the shafts of spears.

T F 5. Snowhouses were built from blocks of soil and vegetation cut from the frozen ground.

T F 6. The Inuit were made up of several different Native American tribes, including the Cherokee, the Huron, and the Mohawk.

T F 7. The Iroquois became famous for living in long houses.

T F 8. Sometimes the Iroquois surrounded their villages with walls made of tree trunks sunk into the ground for protection in times of war.

T F 9. The Ottawain peoples lived near the Ottawa River in east-central Canada.

T F 10. The Algonquin grew some crops, but they were not a farming people.

Directions: Choose two of the false statements from above. Rewrite them on the lines below to make them true.

11. ____

____

12. ____

____

Notes for Home: Your child learned about the early peoples of Canada.
Home Activity: Have your child draw a picture of what he or she thinks early Canadian houses looked like. Discuss with your child the possible advantages and disadvantages of these houses.

Name ______________________ Date __________

Use with Pages 226–227.

Writing Prompt: Adapting to the Environment

The Inuit developed many ways to protect themselves from their harsh environment. People in the United States today also have to protect themselves from their environments. Think about ways people in your community and around the country adapt to the local environment. Write a paragraph explaining how these ways are similar to and different from the Inuit ways?

Notes for Home: Your child learned about the Inuit.
Home Activity: With your child, look for information and pictures of Inuit artifacts on the Internet or at a local library. How are early Inuit artifacts similar to and different from tools used today?

Name ______________________ Date __________

Vocabulary Review

Use with Chapter 8.

Vocabulary Review

Directions: Choose the vocabulary word from the box and write it on the line beside its definition. You may use your glossary.

basin and range	etching	wigwam
tributary	pueblo	temple mound
tundra	adobe	snowhouse
arid	burial mound	sod house
pit house	wattle	long house

_______________ **1.** rectangular building made of logs covered by bark

_______________ **2.** dry

_______________ **3.** made from sun-dried mud

_______________ **4.** framework of twigs, logs, branches, or vines covered with mud

_______________ **5.** dome-shaped frame of branches covered with animal skins or woven mats

_______________ **6.** an imprinted drawing or design

_______________ **7.** cold, treeless land with low-lying vegetation

_______________ **8.** temporary shelter, or igloo, built of blocks cut from snow

_______________ **9.** shelter built from blocks of soil and vegetation cut from the frozen ground

_______________ **10.** smaller stream or river that flows into a larger river

_______________ **11.** hill of dirt used for religious and ceremonial purposes

_______________ **12.** hill of dirt built over the graves of people

_______________ **13.** low area alternating with a small mountain range

_______________ **14.** structure made of adobe bricks

_______________ **15.** shelter made by digging a pit in the ground and covering it with a framework of logs

Notes for Home: Your child learned the vocabulary terms for Chapter 8.
Home Activity: With your child, discuss the different types of shelters listed among the vocabulary terms. Compare and contrast these shelters as you discuss them.

Name ______________________ Date __________

Use with Page 236.

UNIT 3 Project Time Travel

Directions: In a group, host a travel program by presenting a brochure about a historic culture.

1. Our travel program features this culture: ______________________________.

2. The ✔ shows the information included in our travel brochure:

___geography ___leaders ___daily life ___cultural activities ___technology

___economic system ___physical structures ___natural resources ___environment

___other: ______________________________

3. This is how we will describe the historic culture in our travel program:

____

____

____

____

____

____

✔ Checklist for Students

_____ We chose a historic culture.

_____ We made a travel brochure.

_____ We wrote a description and included pictures of our historic culture.

_____ We prepared our travel program.

_____ We presented our travel program and brochure to the class.

Notes for Home: Your child learned about historic cultures.

Home Activity: With your child, read a travel brochure or an article in the travel section of a newspaper or magazine. Make a list of the important features that are included in the description of the place. Which ideas could your child use in his or her travel brochure and program?

Name ______________________ Date ______________ **Reading Social Studies**

Use with Pages 242–243.

Main Idea and Details

Directions: Read the passage. Fill in the circle next to the correct answer.

It did not take long for Alexander to show his leadership qualities. In 334 B.C., just two years after he became king of Macedonia, Alexander successfully invaded the Persian Empire.

In a battle on the plain of Issus in Syria, Alexander showed a real genius for leadership. The much larger Persian army rained a storm of arrows down on Alexander's army. However, Alexander did not order a retreat. Instead, he ordered his army to attack.

When the Persians saw their opponents charging at them, they fled in terror. Alexander was triumphant.

Alexander then turned south. He conquered Syria and Phoenicia (fo NEE shuh). In 332 B.C. he invaded Egypt, where the Persians had ruled for 200 years. The Egyptians quickly surrendered, and Alexander was given the crown of pharaoh.

Alexander now turned back to fight the Persians. In 331 B.C. he once again faced a much larger Persian army. The Persians sent their chariots charging at full speed toward Alexander's army. Alexander ordered his men to stand their ground. Then, at the last moment, his army separated into two groups. The Persian chariots passed right through them. Then Alexander's army closed the line, and the chariots were trapped. The chariots were destroyed. Alexander's army then wiped out the rest of the Persian army.

1. Which of the following is the best main idea of the passage?

Ⓐ The Persian Empire had a great army.
Ⓑ Egyptians were under the rule of the Persian Empire.
Ⓒ Alexander was a brave and clever military leader.
Ⓓ Chariots were a very useful weapon in battle.

2. Which of the following details is NOT true about Alexander's accomplishments as a military leader?

Ⓐ Instead of fleeing from the larger Persian army, Alexander attacked.
Ⓑ Alexander skipped Syria and Phoenicia to attack Egypt.
Ⓒ Alexander was crowned pharaoh of Egypt after the Egyptians' surrender.
Ⓓ In Alexander's second attack on Persia, he trapped and destroyed the Persian chariots.

Notes for Home: Your child learned how to identify the main idea and details of a passage.
Home Activity: With your child, recall a familiar fairy tale, such as "Little Red Riding Hood," "The Three Little Pigs," or another well-known short story. Then work together to identify the main idea and details of the story.

Name ________________________ Date __________ **Vocabulary Preview**

Use with Chapter 9.

Vocabulary Preview

Directions: Fill in the blanks with the words from the box. You may use your glossary.

agora	immortal	marathon	plague
plunder	aristocracy	philosopher	mercenary
myth	democracy	reason	

1. A ____________________ extends human knowledge.

2. Government that is ruled by the people is a ____________________.

3. A fast-spreading, often fatal disease is a ____________________.

4. A hired soldier is called a ____________________.

5. ____________________ is the valuables seized in wartime.

6. The Greek gods could live forever because they were ____________________.

7. The longest race in the Olympics is called a ____________________.

8. Many Greeks would spend their time in an ________________, or an outdoor marketplace.

9. An ____________________ is a form of government controlled by a few wealthy people.

10. To help explain mysteries in nature and life, the Greeks would create a ________________, or a story about the gods and goddesses.

11. ____________________ is the ability to find an explanation for why things happen.

Notes for Home: Your child learned the vocabulary terms for Chapter 9.
Home Activity: Have your child use each vocabulary term in an original sentence.

Name ______________________ Date __________ **Lesson Review**

Use with Pages 246–251.

Lesson 1: The Geography of Greece

The Greek civilization developed in a mountainous region nearly surrounded by seas.

Directions: Fill in the organizer below with facts about ancient Greece. Then answer the questions that follow. You may use your textbook.

Ancient Greece

Climate

1.

2.

Government

1.

Landforms

1.

2.

Entertainment

1.

2.

3.

4.

1. What did the Minoan civilization trade with other islands?

____

2. What made Mycenae so well protected?

____

Notes for Home: Your child learned how the geography of ancient Greece affected its people.
Home Activity: With your child, brainstorm how life in your town might be different if tall mountains kept you isolated from all surrounding cities.

Name ______________________ Date ____________ **Lesson Review**

Use with Pages 252–256.

Lesson 2: The Greek City-States

The Greek city-states of Athens and Sparta were very different.

Directions: Read the following phrases and decide which city-state each one describes. If it is about Sparta, write *S* on the blank line. If it is about Athens, write *A*. Then answer the question that follows. You may use your textbook.

___ **1.** Only healthy infants were allowed to live

___ **2.** Women had more rights than in other city-states

___ **3.** Five hundred citizens formed a council

___ **4.** Strictly ruled military state

___ **5.** Best example of Greek democracy

___ **6.** Boys sent to military camp at age seven

___ **7.** Women had very few rights

___ **8.** Army-centered life

9. Imagine you live in Ancient Greece. Would you rather live in Athens or Sparta? Why?

____

____

____

____

Notes for Home: Your child learned about different ways of life in ancient Greek city-states.
Home Activity: Tell your child that, today, we use the word *spartan* to mean simple, frugal, or severe. Ask him or her how the word may have gotten its meaning. Have your child use *spartan* in an original sentence.

Name ______________________ Date ____________ **Map and Globe Skills**

Use with Pages 258–259.

Compare City Maps at Different Scales

Different maps can show the same location at different scales. The size of the location on the map and the amount of detail included depend upon the map's scale.

Directions: Study the maps and answer the questions that follow in the spaces provided.

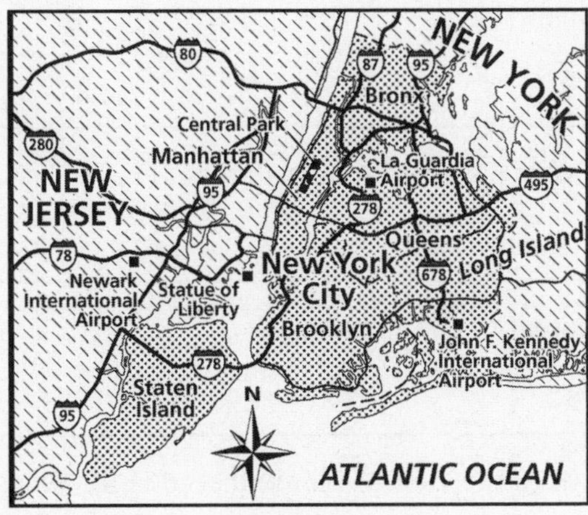

Map A

Map B

1. Which map helps you understand the size of New York City? Explain.

____

____

____

2. Which map helps you understand the general location of Central Park? Explain.

____

____

3. Which map would you use to find your way from John F. Kennedy International Airport to Central Park? Why?

____

____

4. Which map would you use to find your way from the Sheep Meadow to the Reservoir? Why?

____

____

Notes for Home: Your child learned to use maps drawn at different scales.
Home Activity: Using the maps on this page as an example, brainstorm with your child why television news programs, newspapers, and magazines might use maps drawn at different scales.

Name ______________________ Date __________ **Lesson Review**

Use with Pages 260–264.

Lesson 3: The Golden Age of Athens

Directions: Read the following statements. Then write *T* (True) or *F* (False) on the line before each statement. If the answer is false, correct the statement to make it true. You may use your textbook.

____ **1.** In A.D. 490 Persia attacked the Greek mainland.

____

____ **2.** The end of the Persian invasion was soon after a sea battle at Salamis.

____

____ **3.** Athens entered the Golden Age after the defeat of the Persians.

____

____ **4.** During the Golden Age, Greek physicians were the first to blame the gods for illnesses.

____

____ **5.** Athens formed an alliance called the Delian League.

____

____ **6.** During its Golden Age, Sparta became the most powerful Greek city-state.

____

____ **7.** The Athenians destroyed farms to starve Spartans into surrendering.

____

____ **8.** A plague killed thousands of people in Athens.

____

____ **9.** After the war, Sparta was able to regain its military strength.

____

____ **10.** The Spartan army defeated Thebes in 371 B.C.

____

Notes for Home: Your child learned about events during the Golden Age of ancient Athens.
Home Activity: Discuss with your child how the Greeks explained illnesses before and after the Golden Age. Ask how he or she thinks the Athenian plagues might have been explained before the Golden Age.

Name ______________________ Date ____________ **Lesson Review**

Use with Pages 266–271.

Lesson 4: Alexander the Great

Directions: Match each person in the first column with the correct description in the second column. You may use your textbook.

___ **1.** Alexander

___ **2.** Philip II

___ **3.** Hippocrates

___ **4.** Pythagoras

___ **5.** Euclid

___ **6.** Archimedes

a. started a school that led to the development of geometry

b. murdered by a young noble

c. explained how levers work

d. worked out a system of plane geometry

e. took the throne at age 20

f. the "father of medicine"

Directions: Sequence the events that follow from **1** (earliest) to **7** (most recent). You may use your textbook.

___ Alexander invades the Persian Empire.

___ At 33 years of age, Alexander dies before returning home.

___ Alexandria becomes a center for trade and learning.

___ Greek engineers build machines that move heavy loads.

___ Alexander the Great becomes king of Macedonia.

___ The Hellenistic Age begins.

___ The Egyptians surrender.

Notes for Home: Your child learned about the life and accomplishments of Alexander the Great.
Home Activity: With your child, discuss what it might be like to have a 20-year-old President. Research the age requirement for U.S. Presidents and discuss why this restriction may have been created.

Name ____________________ Date __________

Vocabulary Review

Directions: Unscramble the vocabulary word in each sentence to make the sentence true.

1. Thousands of people in Athens died, including Pericles, from a (glupae) ____________.
2. Some city-states were ruled by the people, while others developed into a type of government known as an (sictrrocaya) ____________.
3. Greece is famous for its (mtshy) ____________ about gods and goddesses.
4. A type of race known as a (harmanto) ____________ was named after a plain northeast of Athens.
5. Many Greeks spent their time outdoors in the (raaog) ____________.
6. The best example of a (comedaycr) ____________ in Greece was Athens.
7. In ancient Greece, a person who wanted to explain actions in the world was a (shoroilppeh) ____________.
8. A (encamyrer) ____________ could earn money by fighting against the king of Persia.
9. During the Golden Age, the people of Athens began to respect the power of (serona) ____________.
10. Greek gods and goddesses were much like humans, except they were (toilammr) ____________.
11. The Mycenaeans search for (dulpern) ____________ may have caused a war.

Notes for Home: Your child learned the vocabulary terms for Chapter 9.
Home Activity: After your child has unscrambled all the terms, call out each term and allow him or her to provide the definition.

Name ______________________ Date __________

Vocabulary Preview

Directions: Match each vocabulary word with its meaning. Write the correct letter of the definition on the line next to each word. You may use your glossary.

___ **1.** patrician	**a.** ruler with total control over the people
___ **2.** plebeian	**b.** to rob
___ **3.** republic	**c.** Jewish place of worship
___ **4.** representative	**d.** someone who destroys property
___ **5.** Senate	**e.** sense of pride in one's country
___ **6.** consul	**f.** government where citizens have the right to vote
___ **7.** dictator	**g.** to sell off
___ **8.** tribune	**h.** a follower
___ **9.** patriotism	**i.** leader of the Roman church
___ **10.** caesar	**j.** underground room used as a burial place
___ **11.** emperor	**k.** generally a prisoner or slave who served as a professional fighter
___ **12.** gladiator	**l.** official chosen to manage the government and the army
___ **13.** catacomb	
___ **14.** synagogue	**m.** one elected to represent the people
___ **15.** disciple	**n.** ruler of an empire
___ **16.** persecute	**o.** to punish others for their beliefs
___ **17.** auction	**p.** common Roman citizen with little wealth or power
___ **18.** pope	**q.** Roman ruler
___ **19.** pillage	**r.** person appointed to protect the rights of plebeians
___ **20.** vandal	**s.** wealthy, powerful Roman citizen
	t. governing body

Notes for Home: Your child learned the vocabulary terms for Chapter 10.
Home Activity: Call out each term to your child and have him or her spell it and use it in a sentence.

Name ______________________ Date __________

Lesson Review

Use with Pages 276–279.

Lesson 1: Rome's Beginnings

Directions: Use the description and the map on page 277 to sketch a map of Italy in the box below. Use as much of the box as possible, and label Rome on your drawing. Then answer the questions that follow. You may use your textbook.

1. What island does Italy appear to "kick"?

____

2. Which two crops were popular along the Tiber River?

____

3. What did the early peoples of Italy originally call themselves?

____

4. What did the Romans learn under Etruscan rule?

____

____

Notes for Home: Your child learned about the development of Roman civilization.
Home Activity: With your child, compare his or her drawn map to an actual map of the Mediterranean area. Add cardinal directions to the map and discuss what countries and continents surround Italy.

Name ______________________ Date __________ **Research and Writing Skills**

Use with Pages 280–281.

Use Primary and Secondary Sources

Directions: Read the list of sources below. Write *P* beside each primary source and *S* beside each secondary source. Then, below each item, explain why you classified it as you did. You may use your textbook.

____**1.** book of Roman legends (English translation)

____

____

____**2.** parchment from a Roman trial

____

____

____**3.** statue of Octavian Augustus from 30 B.C.

____

____

____**4.** history book about the Five Good Emperors of Rome

____

____

____**5.** original manuscript of Virgil's *Aeneid*

____

____

____**6.** letter from a Roman tribune to the Senate members

____

____

____ **7.** historian's account of Julius Caesar's victory against Spain

____

____

Notes for Home: Your child learned how to distinguish primary sources from secondary sources.
Home Activity: With your child, analyze examples of writing in your home and determine whether each is a primary or secondary source.

Name ______________________ Date ____________

Lesson Review

Use with Pages 282–287.

Lesson 2: The Roman Republic

Directions: Although daily life in ancient Rome was very different from life today, there were many similarities as well. Compare and contrast Ancient Roman life with your life today. You may use your textbook.

	Ancient Romans' Lives	Life Today
School		
Toys		
Food		
Pets		
Government		

Notes for Home: Your child learned about the daily lives of citizens in ancient Rome.
Home Activity: Ask your child to tell or write his or her daily schedule. Discuss how some of these activities might have differed in ancient Rome.

Name ______________________ Date ____________ **Lesson Review**

Use with Pages 288–292.

Lesson 3: The Roman Empire

Romans were ruled by many different leaders after the death of Julius Caesar.

Directions: Fill out the chart below with information about the emperors of Rome. You may use your textbook.

Emperor	Good or Poor Leader?	Details About Emperor
Augustus		
Caligula		
Claudius		
Nero		
Marcus Aurelius		

Notes for Home: Your child learned about the good and bad emperors of ancient Rome.
Home Activity: With your child, discuss the differences between a republic and an empire. Ask him or her which would be worse, a bad president or a bad emperor and why.

Name ______________________ Date __________ **Lesson Review**

Use with Pages 294–297.

Lesson 4: The Rise of Christianity

Directions: Read the following statements. Then circle *T* (True) or *F* (False) for each statement. If the answer is false, correct the statement to make it true. You may use your textbook.

T F 1. Christianity began with a Jewish man named Jesus.

____

T F 2. Jesus spoke to small groups in homes or Jewish synagogues but never spoke outdoors.

____

T F 3. Ten disciples were chosen to be the Apostles.

____

T F 4. Unlike the Romans, Christians believed in only one God.

____

T F 5. Jesus was arrested for spreading his message.

____

T F 6. The teachings of Jesus spread throughout the Mediterranean region.

____

T F 7. By A.D. 100, Christianity had gained only a few followers in parts of the Roman Empire.

____

T F 8. Constantine, who outlawed the persecution of Christians, died in A.D. 337.

____

T F 9. Christianity was made the official language of Rome in A.D. 337.

____

Notes for Home: Your child learned about the development of Christianity and its effect on the Roman Empire.
Home Activity: With your child, create a chart comparing and contrasting the Greek and Roman gods with the Christians' one God. Ask why the Christians might have been persecuted for their beliefs.

Name ______________________ Date ____________ **Lesson Review**

Use with Pages 298–304.

Lesson 5: Rise and Fall

Directions: Fill in the circle next to each INCORRECT answer. You may use your textbook.

1. Commodus ______________________.

Ⓐ ruled as emperor of Rome
Ⓑ was a caring leader
Ⓒ loved spending money
Ⓓ performed as a gladiator

2. Emperor Diocletian ______________________.

Ⓐ reigned from 284 to 305 B.C.
Ⓑ introduced new reforms
Ⓒ helped restore order to the empire
Ⓓ controlled the empire with a "co-emperor"

3. Constantinople ______________________.

Ⓐ was first called New Rome
Ⓑ became the center of the Byzantine Empire
Ⓒ was named after the Greek city Byzantium
Ⓓ was built in the eastern part of the Roman Empire

4. The Visigoths ______________________.

Ⓐ were led by Alaric
Ⓑ pillaged Rome in A.D. 410
Ⓒ rode horses into the homes of the wealthy
Ⓓ buried what they could not take with them

5. As Rome declined ______________________.

Ⓐ Constantinople became the center of Roman power
Ⓑ the Byzantine Empire became more prosperous
Ⓒ the Byzantine Empire kept its power for another 1,000 years
Ⓓ Romulus Augustus became leader of the Byzantine Empire

Notes for Home: Your child learned about the rise and fall of the Roman Empire.
Home Activity: With your child, compare and contrast the leadership characteristics of Commodus and Diocletian. Then discuss what traits are found in good leaders.

Vocabulary Review

Directions: Fill in the crossword puzzle with the vocabulary terms from Chapter 10. Not all vocabulary words will be used. You may use your textbook.

Across

2. someone who destroys property
3. a ruler with total control
7. ruler of an empire
8. sense of pride in one's country
10. underground tomb
11. a follower
13. to punish others for their beliefs

Down

1. professional fighter
4. to sell off
5. government where citizens choose the leaders
6. one elected to office by the people
9. Jewish place of worship
10. official who manages the government and the army
12. to rob

Notes for Home: Your child learned the vocabulary terms for Chapter 10.
Home Activity: Have your child create a word-search puzzle for you to complete. Tell him or her to position the vocabulary words in the puzzle and to use their definitions as clues.

Name ______________________ Date __________

Discovery Channel School

Use with Page 312.

Unit 4 Project Feature Film

Directions: In a group, write a screenplay and bring a Greek myth to life.

1. Our Greek myth is ______________________________________.
2. The list of characters (including a narrator):

   ____________________ ____________________

   ____________________ ____________________

   ____________________ ____________________
3. The setting and location: ______________________________
4. Use a separate sheet of paper for the following exercises:
   - Write an introduction for your story.
   - Describe the different scenes from your story.
   - Write dialogue for the characters.
   - Write instructions for a camera or tape recorder operator.
   - Create special effects for the screenplay. Include a backdrop or music and sound effects.
5. Perform your Greek myth for the class.

✔ Checklist for Students

_____ We chose a Greek myth.

_____ We chose the characters, setting, and location.

_____ We wrote a story introduction.

_____ We wrote the characters' dialogue.

_____ We wrote instructions for a camera or tape recorder operator.

_____ We performed our screenplay for the class.

Notes for Home: Your child learned about Greek myths.
Home Activity: With your child, discuss Greek myths with which you are familiar. Share details about each myth, including the setting, important characters, and a summary of the plot.

Name ________________________ Date ________ **Reading Social Studies**

Use with Pages 318-319.

Sequence

Directions: Read the passage. Then answer the questions that follow.

Kublai Khan, grandson of Mongol leader Genghis Khan, was born in 1215. Between 1252 and 1259, Kublai Khan was a military leader who helped his brother, Mangu Khan, try to conquer China. After his brother died in 1259, Kublai defeated another brother, Arigh Boki, for control of the government. Kublai finally was named Khan, or ruler, in 1260.

By 1280, Kublai Khan had conquered southern China and Burma and eventually controlled all of China. This conquest established the Mongol dynasty.

Under the rule of Kublai Khan, culture, literature, and the arts flourished. People enjoyed religious freedom. Kublai Khan also increased the use of postal stations, replaced coins with paper money, made roadway improvements, and expanded waterways.

Later, after two failed attempts to invade Japan, Kublai Khan's rule began to decline. He died in 1294, having left his mark on China.

1. Which event took place first?
- Ⓐ Kublai Khan invaded Japan.
- Ⓑ Kublai Khan invaded southern China.
- Ⓒ The Mongol dynasty promoted freedom of religion.
- Ⓓ Arigh Boki was defeated.

2. Which clue word in the passage indicates that Kublai Khan was named ruler following the death of his brother?
- Ⓐ initially
- Ⓑ before
- Ⓒ after
- Ⓓ first

3. Which event took place last?
- Ⓐ The Mongol dynasty was established.
- Ⓑ Kublai Khan conquered southern China.
- Ⓒ Arigh Boki and Kublai Khan battled for control.
- Ⓓ Arigh Boki was defeated by his brother.

Notes for Home: Your child learned to identify clue words that signal the sequence of the events in a passage.
Home Activity: Relate to your child an experience from your life. Use the clue words *before, initially, after, later,* and *finally* and specific dates to sequence the details.

Name ______________________ Date __________

Use with Chapter 11.

Vocabulary Preview

Directions: Read each sentence. Then replace the words in italics with a vocabulary word from the box and write it on the line provided. You may use your glossary.

hippodrome	icon	caravan	astrolabe
cathedral	pilgrimage	mosque	

1. Many Muslims plan to make a *journey to a place of religious importance* to Mecca one time in their life.

   ____

2. A disagreement over the use of an *image of Jesus or a saint* as part of worship led to a split in the Christian church in 1054.

   ____

3. Muslim astronomers used an *instrument to map the stars in the sky* to determine directions.

   ____

4. In medieval Arabia a *group of people and animals traveling together* was a common sight.

   ____

5. The Hagia Sophia is an example of a *large, important Christian church.*

   ____

6. The *ancient Greek stadium used for horse and chariot racing* in Constantinople was the center of entertainment.

   ____

7. Five daily prayers are offered in a *Muslim place of worship.*

   ____

Notes for Home: Your child learned the vocabulary terms for Chapter 11.
Home Activity: With your child, write a story about the Byzantine Empire using all of the vocabulary words correctly.

Name ______________________ Date ____________ **Lesson Review**

Use with Pages 322-325.

Lesson 1: Geography of the Byzantine Empire

Directions: Read the following statements. Then write *T* (True) or *F* (False) on the line before each statement. If the answer is false, correct the statement to make it true. You may use your textbook.

1. ___ In the southern and eastern European parts of the Byzantine Empire, people enjoyed mild, rainy summers and cool, wet winters.

____

2. ___ Farmers raised such crops as grapes, olives, wheat, and barley.

____

3. ___ In the southern and eastern European parts of the Byzantine Empire, most people lived in large cities.

____

4. ___ The desert regions in the Byzantine Empire received heavy rainfall.

____

5. ___ People in northern Africa and across much of southwestern Asia lived their entire lives in the same town.

____

6. ___ Constantinople was renamed Byzantium.

____

7. ___ Constantinople was protected on three sides by water.

____

8. ___ Constantinople was the entertainment center of the Byzantine Empire.

____

9. ___ The Byzantine Empire crumbled before the Roman Empire.

____

Notes for Home: Your child learned how the geography of the Byzantine Empire influenced the people who lived there.
Home Activity: With your child, discuss how physical features and climate affect people in your community.

Name ______________________ Date ____________

Lesson Review

Use with Pages 326–328.

Lesson 2: The Greatness of the Byzantine Empire

During the rule of Justinian, the Byzantine Empire reached its height.

Directions: Fill in the organizer below with facts about life during Justinian's rule. You may use your textbook.

Religion

1.

2.

3.

Law

1.

2.

3.

Rule of Justinian I

Art and Architecture

1.

2.

3.

Politics

1.

2.

3.

Notes for Home: Your child learned about the rule of Justinian.
Home Activity: With your child, discuss why it is important to have an organized, written code of law.

Name ______________________ Date ____________ **Lesson Review**

Use with Pages 330-333.

Lesson 3: Development of Islam

Directions: Match each person or term in the first column with the correct description in the second column.

___ **1.** Mecca	**a.** the holy book of Islam
___ **2.** Islam	**b.** founder of the religion Islam
___ **3.** Muhammad	**c.** religious duty in Islam
___ **4.** Quran	**d.** holy city of Islam
___ **5.** Muslim	**e.** five basic duties of Muslims
___ **6.** "Pillars of Islam"	**f.** believer in Islam
___ **7.** jihad	**g.** religion revealed to Muhammad

Directions: Reread the Five Pillars on pp. 332–333 of your textbook and summarize each duty in your own words in the chart below.

First pillar	
Second pillar	
Third pillar	
Fourth pillar	
Fifth pillar	

Notes for Home: Your child learned about the establishment of Islam and some of its basic principles.
Home Activity: Discuss with your child the role religious beliefs play in your family. In what religious customs and celebrations do you participate?

Name ______________________ Date ____________ **Lesson Review**

Use with Pages 334-338.

Lesson 4: The Islamic World

Muslim traders and travelers exchanged ideas and technology throughout the empire and with different parts of the world.

Directions: Look at each innovation listed in the first column of the chart. Complete the chart by identifying the advantages of these innovations to Muslims in the 1300s and to society today.

Innovations	Advantages to Muslims	Advantages Today
Branch banking		
Irrigation systems		
Algebra		
Astronomy		
Mapmaking		
Medical encyclopedia		

Notes for Home: Your child learned how trade helped spread ideas and technology throughout the Islamic world and the rest of the world.

Home Activity: With your child, discuss which of the innovations in the chart have had the greatest impact on the world. Support your choice with modern-day examples.

Name ______________________ Date __________ **Chart and Graph Skills**

Use with Pages 340–341.

Interpret Line Graphs

Line graphs show how a measurement changes as time passes. **Directions:** Study the line graph about the number of people who have made a pilgrimage to Mecca since 1950. Then answer the questions that follow.

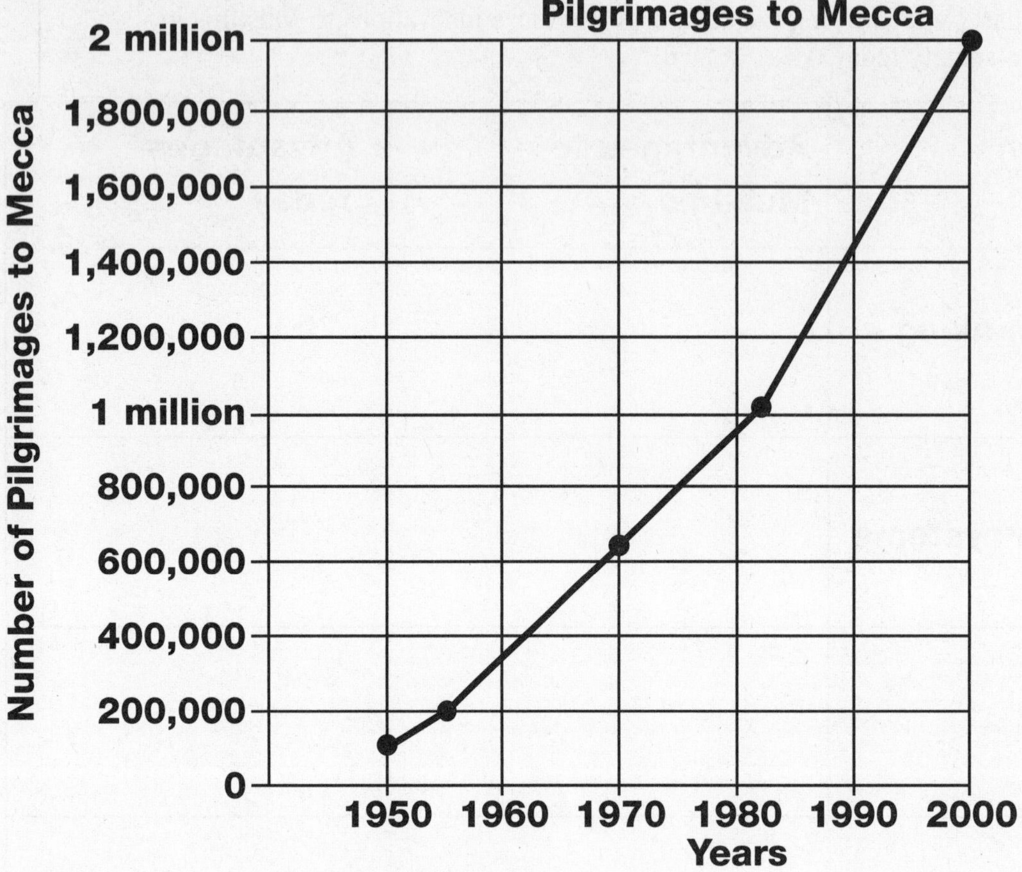

1. What time span does this graph cover?

____

2. About how many pilgrimages were made to Mecca in 1983?

____

3. What trend does this graph show, and what do you think is the reason?

____

____

____

____

Notes for Home: Your child learned to use line graphs.
Home Activity: With your child, use the Internet or community resources to make a line graph plotting changes in population in your community between 1950 and 2000. What trend does your data show?

Name ______________________ Date __________ **Vocabulary Review**

Use with Chapter 11.

Vocabulary Review

Directions: Use the vocabulary words from Chapter 11 to complete each item. Use the numbered letters to answer the clue that follows.

hippodrome	icon	caravan	astrolabe
cathedral	pilgrimage	mosque	

1. Ancient Greek stadium for horse and chariot racing ___ (3) ___ (6) ___
2. Large or important Christian church ___ (8) ___
3. Image of Jesus or a saint ___
4. Journey to a place of religious importance ___ (1) ___
5. Group of people and animals traveling together ___ (7) ___
6. Muslim house of worship (5) ___ (2) ___
7. Instrument to map the stars in the sky (4) ___

Clue: This prophet from Mecca founded the religion of Islam.

___ ___ ___ ___ ___ ___ ___ ___
1 2 3 4 5 6 7 8

Notes for Home: Your child learned the vocabulary terms for Chapter 11.
Home Activity: Have your child write sentences using each vocabulary word or make vocabulary cards and practice saying the definitions together.

Name ______________________ Date __________ **Vocabulary Preview**

Use with Chapter 12.

Vocabulary Preview

Directions: Circle the vocabulary term that best completes each sentence. Then write the definition of that word on the lines provided. You may use your glossary.

1. A (samurai, daimyo, shogun) was a ruler who governed large areas of farmland.

____

____

2. A (snow storm, typhoon, drought) is most likely to occur at sea.

____

____

3. A person who held a special, high-ranking military office in early Japan was a (samurai, daimyo, shogun).

____

____

4. An (aristocrat, samurai, shogun) is a member of a high social class.

____

____

5. A (samurai, daimyo, shogun) was a warrior who defended the land and kept order in society.

____

____

Notes for Home: Your child learned the vocabulary terms for Chapter 12.
Home Activity: Have your child use these terms to tell you about society in early Japan.

Name ______________________ Date __________ **Lesson Review**

Use with Pages 346–349.

Lesson 1: Empire of Asia

Directions: Circle the response that best completes each sentence. You may use your textbook.

1. Asia covers about (one-fourth, one-third, one-half) of Earth's land surface.
2. One ocean that does not border Asia is the (Indian Ocean, Pacific Ocean, Atlantic Ocean, Arctic Ocean).
3. The climate of Asia (varies greatly, varies somewhat, is the same) from region to region.
4. Most Asians live (in mountain ranges, in river or mountain valleys, in the desert).
5. The most important economic activity in Asia is (trade, manufacturing, agriculture).

Directions: Compare and contrast Mogul emperors Akbar and Aurangzeb by completing the following chart.

	Akbar	**Aurangzeb**
How did the emperor treat non-Muslims?		
How well did the emperor control the government? How do you know?		
Brought or kept what area under Mogul control?		

Notes for Home: Your child learned the role landforms and climate played in the growth of the Mogul Empire.
Home Activity: With your child, trace Asia's important rivers on the map on p. 347. Then look at the physical map of the United States in an atlas. How does the flow of major rivers affect how and where people live?

Name ______________________ Date ____________ **Lesson Review**

Use with Pages 350–355.

Lesson 2: Chinese Dynasties

Directions: Match each dynasty in the box below to its achievement, accomplishment, or description. Write the name of the dynasty on the line. You will use each dynasty more than once. You may use your textbook.

Sui	Tang	Song	Mongol	Ming

1. __________ China ruled by non-Chinese ruler for first time

2. __________ Military used gunpowder for first time

3. __________ Great advancements made in exploration

4. __________ Literature and fine arts flourished

5. __________ High taxes and forced labor caused collapse of dynasty

6. __________ Improvements made in conquered lands

7. __________ Improvements made in iron production, agriculture, and construction

8. __________ China isolated from the rest of the world

9. __________ System of connected waterways established

10. __________ Trade increased with Central and western Asia

11. __________ Improved road and water travel for traders

12. __________ First to use fractions

13. __________ China led the world in sailing expertise

14. __________ Reinforced and extended Great Wall for protection

15. __________ China ruled by its first female ruler, Wu Hou

Notes for Home: Your child learned about the contributions of medieval Chinese dynasties to trade and technology.

Home Activity: With your child, review the Fact File on p. 351 of achievements and advancements during early Chinese dynasties. Discuss one achievement each of you considers to have had the greatest impact on the world.

Name ______________________ Date ____________

Lesson Review

Use with Pages 356-359.

Lesson 3: The Khmer

Directions: Use complete sentences to answer the following questions. You may use your textbook.

1. Where was the Khmer kingdom located?

____

____

2. Which culture was a major influence on the Khmer civilization?

____

____

3. Why was it valuable for a Khmer ruler to be a deva-raja?

____

____

4. Why was the irrigation system important to the Khmer economy?

____

____

____

5. What do you think is meant by a "golden age" of a civilization?

____

____

____

6. For what purpose was the Angkor Wat built? In what ways is it the same and different today?

____

____

____

____

Notes for Home: Your child learned about the Khmer kingdom in Southeast Asia.
Home Activity: With your child, discuss the importance of a national symbol to a people, such as the symbolism of the Angkor Wat to the Khmer.

Name ______________________ Date __________ **Lesson Review**

Use with Pages 360-363.

Lesson 4: Japan in Isolation

Directions: Sequence the following events in the order in which they took place by numbering them from *1* (earliest) to *10* (most recent). You may use your textbook.

___ Shogun Tokugawa Ieyasu rose to power.

___ The merchant class grew.

___ Nobles worked to weaken the emperor's power.

___ The class system began to crumble.

___ The Mongols in China made two attempts to invade and conquer Japan.

___ Japan's states were united under the country's first constitution.

___ Edo became a large city.

___ Foreigners were forced out of Japan.

___ Japan fell into a long civil war.

___ A four-class system was enforced under shogun rule.

Directions: Complete the cause-and-effect chart by identifying three effects of the shogun's control of trade in Japan in the 1600s.

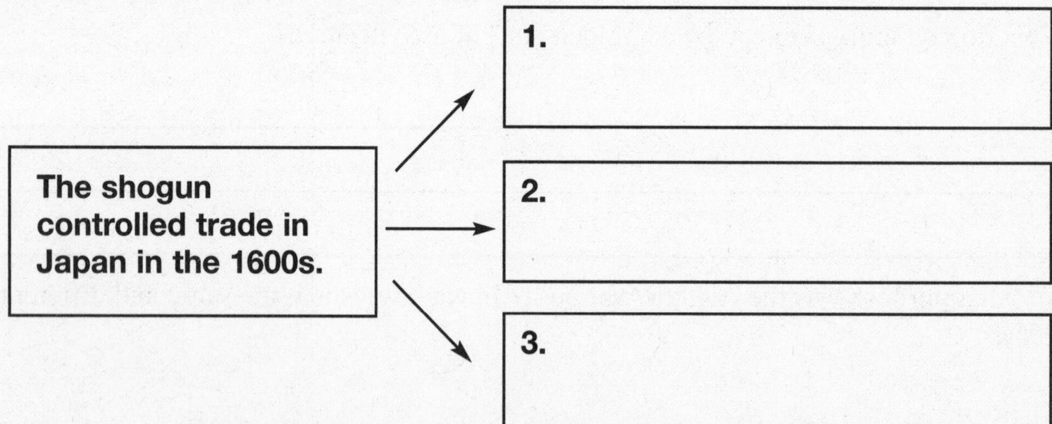

Notes for Home: Your child learned about early Japan and its policy of isolation in the 1600s.
Home Activity: During this period, Japanese scholars learned about world events from foreign books. With your child, discuss international events that influence the United States and how we learn about them.

Name ______________________ Date ____________

Research and Writing Skills

Use with Pages 364-365.

Gather and Report Information

Directions: Review the list of print and online sources in the box below and read each of the following topics about Japan. Identify in which sources you might look for information on each subject and write the sources on the lines provided. Not all sources will be used. Answers to each topic are located at the bottom of the page.

almanac	gazetteer	magazine or periodical
atlas	geographical dictionary	primary source
biographical dictionary	encyclopedia	thesaurus
dictionary	newspaper	yearbook

1. Number of years shoguns ruled in Japan

   Possible Sources: ____________________

2. Distance between Tokyo and Kyoto

   Possible Sources: ____________________

3. Number of main islands in Japan

   Possible Sources: ____________________

4. Meaning of *emperor*

   Possible Sources: ____________________

5. When Edo was founded

   Possible Sources: ____________________

6. Languages spoken by Crown Princess Masako

   Possible Sources: ____________________

Answers: 1. About 700 years; **2.** About 230 miles; **3.** Four; **4.** Ruler of an empire; **5.** Around 1456; **6.** Japanese, English, French, German.

Notes for Home: Your child learned to gather and report information.
Home Activity: With your child, create a short news program with your child as the news anchor. Gather and report information that has been in the news for the past few days.

Name ______________________ Date __________

Vocabulary Review

Directions: Use each of the vocabulary terms from Chapter 12 in an original sentence. Write the sentences on the lines provided. You may use your glossary.

1. aristocrat

____

____

2. samurai

____

____

3. typhoon

____

____

4. daimyo

____

____

5. shogun

____

____

Notes for Home: Your child learned the vocabulary terms for Chapter 12.
Home Activity: Have your child explain how these five terms are related to Japan and the role the shoguns played in the evolution of social classes in Japan.

Name ______________________ Date ____________ **Vocabulary Preview**

Use with Chapter 13.

Vocabulary Preview

Directions: Choose the vocabulary word from the box and write it on the line beside its definition. You may use your textbook. Then use each word in an original sentence on the lines provided.

savanna	griot	Swahili	oba

1. ____________ professional storyteller

____

____

2. ____________ king in Benin

____

____

3. ____________ both a language and a culture; combination of Muslim and East African cultures

____

____

4. ____________ short, grassy plains

____

____

Notes for Home: Your child learned the vocabulary terms for Chapter 13.
Home Activity: Work together with your child to use these terms and details in the chapter to tell a story about African culture.

Name ______________________ Date ____________ **Lesson Review**

Use with Pages 370-373.

Lesson 1: The Geography of Africa

Directions: Decide whether each detail describes a desert, savanna, rain forest, or Mediterranean climate zone in Africa. For desert write a *D* in the blank, for savanna write an *S,* for rain forest write an *R,* and for Mediterranean write an *M.* Then answer the questions that follow. You may use your textbook.

___ **1.** about half of Africa

___ **2.** mostly hot summers

___ **3.** thick vegetation

___ **4.** hot and dry

___ **5.** suitable for agriculture

___ **6.** south of the Sahara

___ **7.** little vegetation and few animals

___ **8.** farming nearly impossible

___ **9.** covers a very small area of the continent

___ **10.** generally mild and rainy winters

___ **11.** the Sahara

12. What made the journeys across Africa dangerous?

____

____

____

13. Why did people migrate to other areas of Africa?

____

____

Notes for Home: Your child learned how the geography of Africa affects its people.
Home Activity: Select a climate zone discussed in this chapter. With your child, compare and contrast characteristics of its climate to the climate where you live.

Name ____________________ Date ____________ **Lesson Review**

Use with Pages 374-378.

Lesson 2: West African Kingdoms

Ghana, Mali, and Songhai were wealthy kingdoms in West Africa.

Directions: Complete the outline with information from this lesson about these empires. You may use your textbook.

I. Ghana

A. People

1. Religion of ____________
2. Adopted Arabic system of ____________

B. Economy and Trade

1. ______________________________ for a living
2. Capital city ____________, major center of trade

C. Political Rule

1. Founded by____________, who ____________________ empire by 1203

II. Mali

A. People

1. An Arab ____________ built mosques, and ____________ brought Muslim learning
2. ____________, oldest known city in sub-Saharan Africa: 200 B.C. to A.D. 1400

B. Economy and Trade

1. Strong ____________ economy, but relied on ____________ for wealth

C. Political Rule

1. ____________ greatest king, took pilgrimage to ____________

III. Songhai

A. People

1. ____________ among different Muslim groups contributed to end of empire

B. Economy and Trade

1. Bigger center of ________________ than Mali

C. Political Rule

1. ____________, important king who divided land into ____________
2. Professional ______________ protected kingdom, defeated by ______________

Notes for Home: Your child learned about three empires of West Africa.
Home Activity: With your child, review the information in this outline. Together, create a Venn diagram to compare and contrast the empires of Ghana, Mali, and Songhai.

Name ______________________ Date __________

Lesson Review

Use with Pages 380-385.

Lesson 3: East, Central, and Southern Africa

Directions: Match the places in the box to the clues and write the terms on the lines provided. You will use each term more than once. You may use your textbook.

Axum	Ethiopia	Kilwa	Great Zimbabwe	Benin

1. exported ivory, frankincense, and myrrh ______________________

2. destroyed by change in climate and trade routes ______________________

3. known for its great art ______________________

4. used Swahili to help traders communicate ______________________

5. ruled by Solomonids after overthrow of Zagwe dynasty ______________________

6. ruled by kings called obas ______________________

7. replaced Axum civilization ______________________

8. attacked by Portuguese for control of Indian Ocean trade ______________________

9. ruled by Ezana ______________________

10. abandoned when population exhausted resources ______________________

11. built several churches out of solid rock ______________________

12. gained wealth by taxing trade goods ______________________

13. located in a fertile forest region near Niger River ______________________

14. built stone enclosures to show king's power ______________________

Notes for Home: Your child learned about trading empires in eastern, central, and southern Africa.
Home Activity: With your child, discuss the importance of trade to your community and state. What resources does your community sell to other places?

Name ______________________ Date __________

Use the Internet

The Internet contains millions of pages of information on all kinds of topics. You can access the Internet through your computer and use a search engine to help you find information on a particular topic. **Directions:** Answer the following questions about using the Internet on the lines provided.

1. Why do you think it can be helpful to use a search engine when looking for information on the Internet?

____

____

2. What is one advantage of researching a topic on the Internet?

____

____

3. What is one disadvantage of researching a topic on the Internet?

____

4. What keywords might you type in to locate information about Mansa Musa's journey to the Middle East?

____

____

Directions: Complete the flowchart by using the terms in the box to sequence the steps for using a search engine.

Select a search engine.	Narrow your topic, if necessary.	Choose a topic.
Type in the keywords.	Access the Internet.	

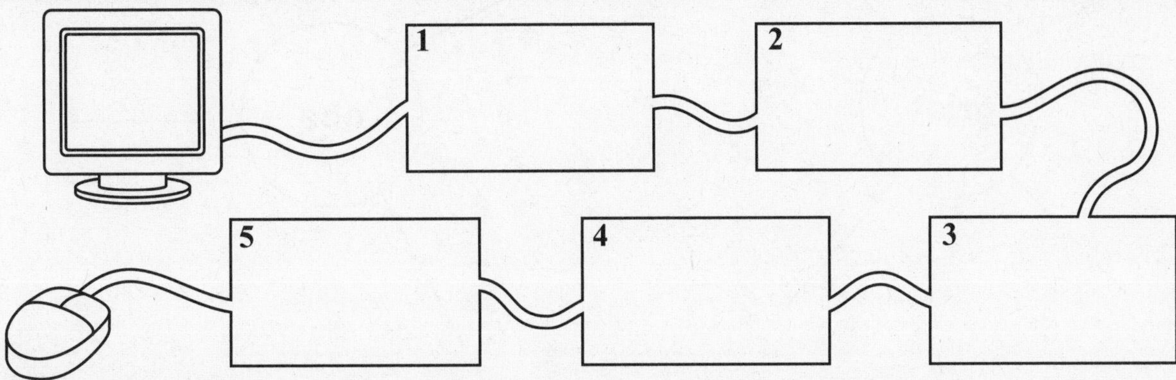

Notes for Home: Your child learned how to use search engines on the Internet.
Home Activity: With your child, practice using various Internet search engines on a home or library computer to research a topic of interest.

Name ____________________ Date __________

Vocabulary Review

Use with Chapter 13.

Vocabulary Review

Directions: Match each term or description in the box below to a vocabulary word from this chapter. Write the term or description on a line on the concept maps.

trading language	tells about life of Sundiata	ruled powerful empire
storyteller	about half of Africa	south of the Sahara
"people of the coast"	lived in a beautiful palace	kingdom of Benin
people herd cattle	empire of Mali	king
fertile soil	African and Muslim cultures	climate zone
culture and language		oral stories

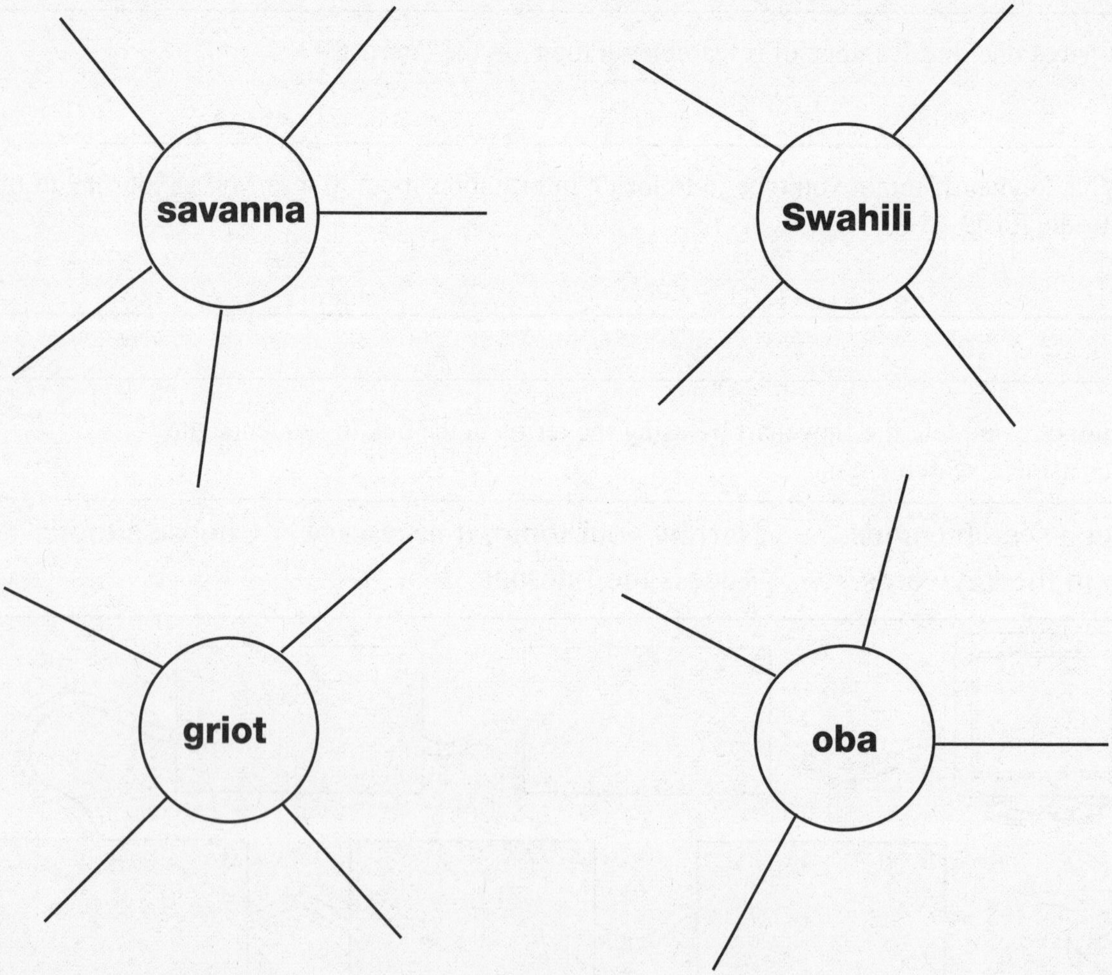

savanna

Swahili

griot

oba

Notes for Home: Your child learned the vocabulary terms for Chapter 13.
Home Activity: After your child has categorized all the terms, verbally summarize for your child the information recorded in each concept map. Have your child listen carefully and correct any errors noticed in your summary.

Vocabulary Preview

Directions: Circle the word that best completes each sentence. You may use your textbook.

1. A baker, goldsmith, tailor, or weaver might have joined a craft (epidemic, guild, monarch) to unite common interests.

2. The (lady, monarch, serf) was the supreme ruler at the top of the feudalism social structure.

3. A (knight, serf, lady) was someone who farmed the land owned by the lords.

4. A man who devoted his life to religion was called a (monk, nun, monarch).

5. A (monastery, convent, missionary) served as a center of religion and education for the nuns who lived there.

6. A trained warrior in the third level in the feudalism pyramid was called a (knight, monarch, guild).

7. A (serf, lady, knight) was of noble birth but had little opportunity to make life decisions without direction from a spouse.

8. In addition to prayer and studies, a (lady, knight, nun), or woman devoted to religion, also cultivated crops and helped the poor.

9. The Plague was an aggressive (epidemic, monarch, guild) that killed about 25 percent of Europe's people in about five years.

10. According to a code of (guild, chivalry, missionary), a knight pledged to use his strength to stand against injustice.

11. A (missionary, knight, monastery) teaches a religion to people with different beliefs.

12. Monks studied, prayed, and lived in a community called a (convent, monastery, monarch).

Notes for Home: Your child learned the vocabulary terms for Chapter 14.
Home Activity: Have your child write each vocabulary word on a slip of paper and copy the definition on the back. Laying each paper with the term facing up, help your child define each word.

Name ______________________ Date __________

Lesson Review

Use with Pages 392-395.

Lesson 1: Geography of Europe

The climate and landforms across Europe affect where and how people live.

Directions: Review each term in the box below. Copy the terms into the correct section of the organizer to describe the four major land regions of Europe. Some terms will be used more than once.

pastureland	mountains	vast area
rocky soil	steep slopes	fertile farming
forests	flat, rolling land	thin soil
		poor farming

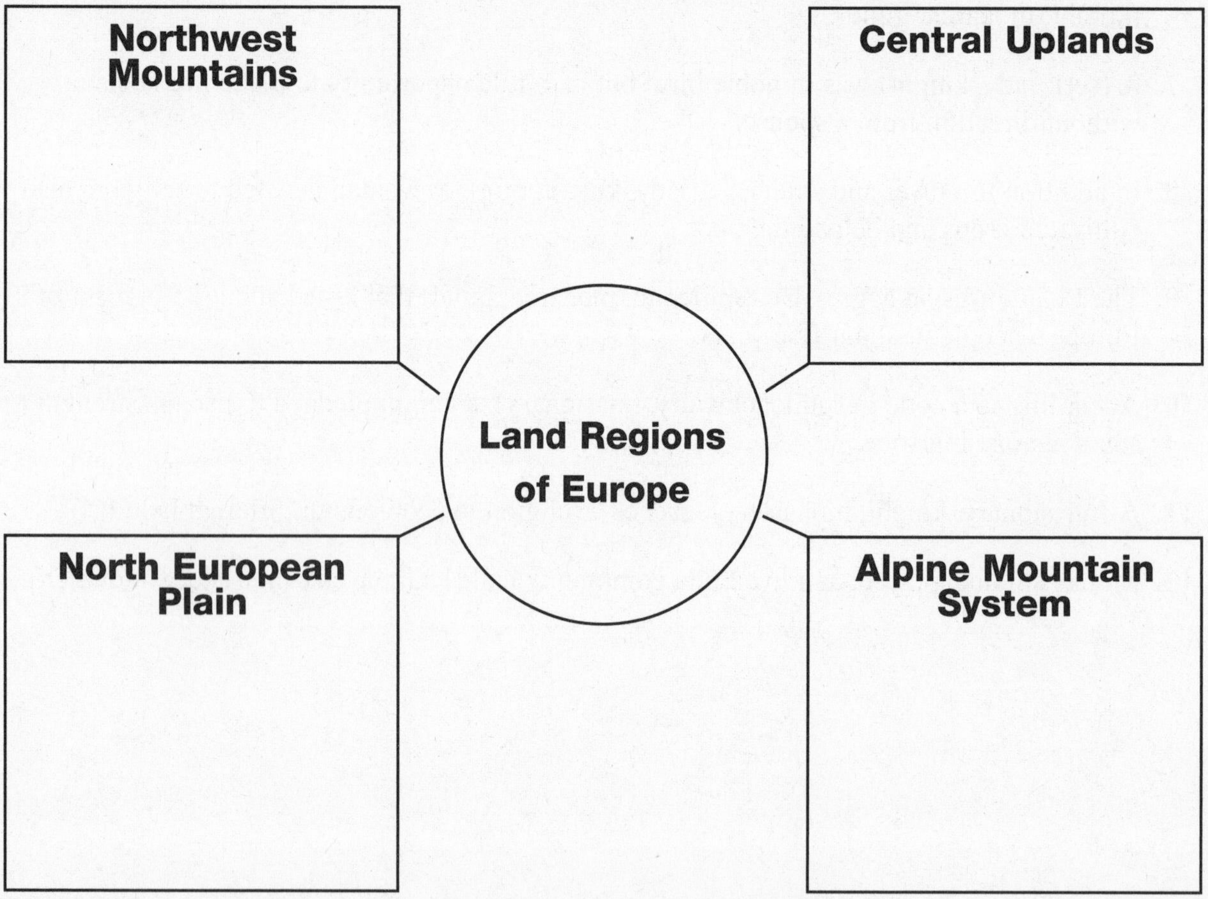

Northwest Mountains

Central Uplands

Land Regions of Europe

North European Plain

Alpine Mountain System

Notes for Home: Your child learned about the climate and landforms of Europe.
Home Activity: With your child, discuss how the climate and landforms where you live affect how people live and work. Then compare your region to the four land regions of Europe.

Name ____________________ Date __________ **Lesson Review**

Use with Pages 396-398.

Lesson 2: Rulers and Invaders

Directions: Match each phrase in Column A to the phrase in Column B that best completes the sentence. Write the letter from Column B on the line in front of Column A. You may use your textbook.

Column A

___ **1.** Before the Domesday Book was put together in 1086,

___ **2.** Because Charlemagne gave large areas of land to the nobles,

___ **3.** Despite Charlemagne's efforts to strengthen his kingdom,

___ **4.** After the Vikings looted the lands they conquered,

___ **5.** After the Normans settled in northern France,

___ **6.** Because King John governed with more force than earlier kings did,

___ **7.** After King John lost an important battle against France,

___ **8.** Rather than face defeat in England's civil war,

___ **9.** Although most of the clauses of the Magna Carta helped the lords and other landholders,

___ **10.** When King John agreed to the set of promises in the Magna Carta,

Column B

a. it fell apart after his death.

b. they were loyal to him and maintained roads, bridges, and defense walls on their estates.

c. civil war broke out in England.

d. they set up trading centers and trade routes.

e. no one really knew how many people lived in England.

f. some of the articles eventually helped all people.

g. royal power was limited.

h. English lords became angry with his rule.

i. they adopted Frankish customs and became Christians and church leaders.

j. King John agreed to the Magna Carta.

Notes for Home: Your child learned about medieval government in Europe under different rulers and invaders.
Home Activity: Review the articles of the Magna Carta discussed on p. 398. With your child, review the rules you have at home. Discuss why rules exist and why they are valuable.

Name ______________________ Date ____________ **Lesson Review**

Use with Pages 400-405.

Lesson 3: Life in the Middle Ages

Directions: Complete the concept map below. Classify each description in the box by listing it in one of the levels of feudalism. You may use your textbook.

received land from the lord	kings or queens	granted estates to lords
gave military support	protected serfs	no loyalty to monarchs or lords
trained to fight on horseback	supreme rulers	followed code of behavior
owned land and crops	peasants	
	lived on and farmed the land	

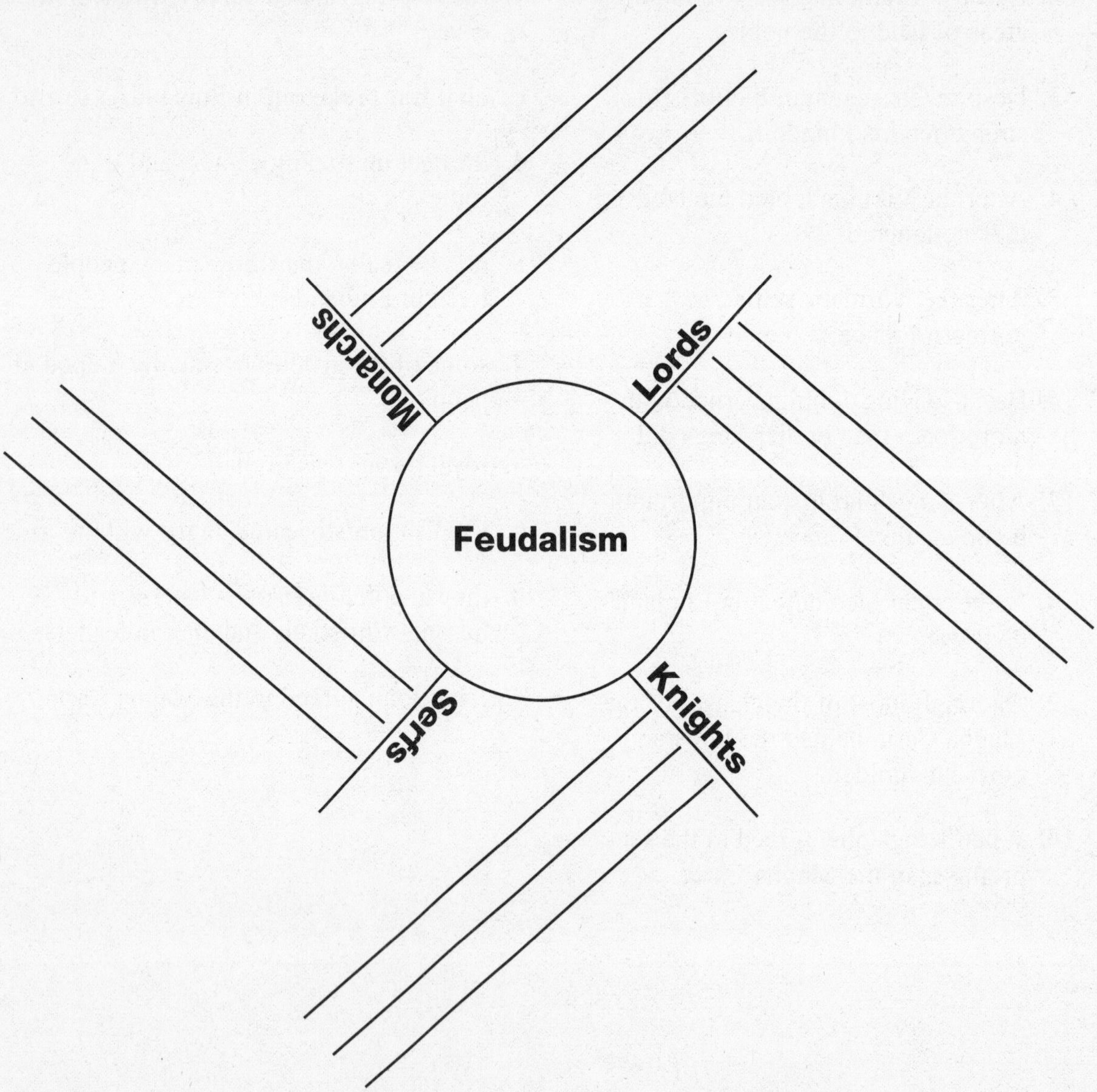

Feudalism

Monarchs

Lords

Serfs

Knights

Notes for Home: Your child learned about feudalism in Europe during the Middle Ages.
Home Activity: With your child, compare how feudalism provided protection for people in medieval Europe and how people in democracies are protected today.

Name ______________________ Date ____________

Lesson Review

Use with Pages 406-411.

Lesson 4: Crusades, Trade, and the Plague

Directions: Read the following statements. Then circle *T* (True) or *F* (False) for each statement. If the answer is false, correct the statement to make it true. You may use your textbook.

T F 1. Christians in western Europe organized twelve Crusades to establish trade routes and defeat the Byzantine Empire.

____

____

T F 2. Because people began to want goods that were not available on a manor, they purchased the goods at fairs.

____

____

T F 3. If traders wanted goods from Asia, they had to travel to Asia to buy them.

____

____

T F 4. The Silk Road is a single route across Central Asia.

____

____

T F 5. Some historians believe that the Plague began in Central Asia and spread east to China and west along the Silk Road.

____

____

T F 6. The Plague killed about three-fourths of Europe's people from 1347 to 1352.

____

____

Notes for Home: Your child learned about the development of trade routes and their effect on communication between Europe, Africa, and Asia.
Home Activity: With your child, compare how epidemics from the Middle Ages and today are spread and are contained.

Name ______________________ Date ____________

Use with Pages 412–413.

Use a Time Zone Map

A time zone map of the United States shows six of the world's time zones. The time in each zone is different by one hour from the time zone next to it. When it is 5 A.M. in Hawaii, it is 8 A.M. in Phoenix, 9 A.M. in Dallas, and 10 A.M. in Washington, D.C.

Directions: Use the time zone map of the United States to answer the questions that follow.

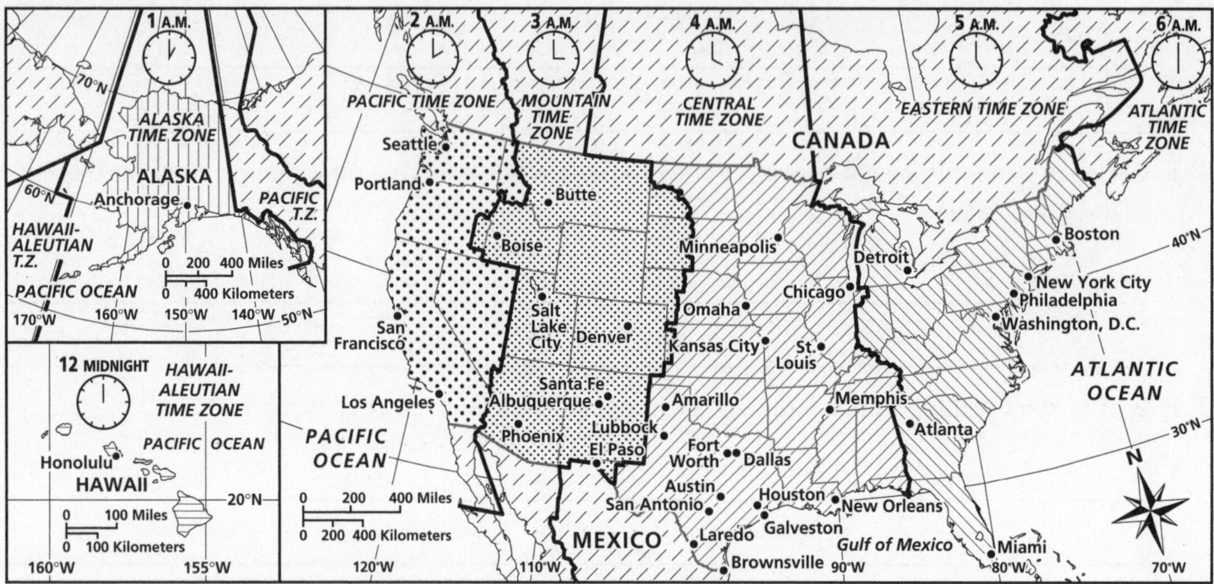

1. Suppose you are about to fly from Albuquerque, New Mexico, to Dallas, Texas. It is about a two-hour flight to Dallas and the plane is scheduled to depart at 10:00 A.M. About what time will you arrive in Dallas?

   Ⓐ 12:00 P.M. Ⓑ 12:00 A.M. Ⓒ 1:00 P.M. Ⓓ 11:00 A.M.

2. Suppose it is 10:30 A.M. in Anchorage, Alaska. What time is it in Chicago, Illinois?

   Ⓐ 11:30 A.M. Ⓑ 12:30 A.M. Ⓒ 12:00 P.M. Ⓓ 1:30 P.M.

3. Suppose you live in Chicago, Illinois, and you want to call a friend in California at 6:00 P.M. Pacific time. At what time in Chicago should you make the call?

   Ⓐ 6:00 P.M. Ⓑ 7:00 P.M. Ⓒ 8:00 P.M. Ⓓ 9:00 P.M.

4. Suppose you are in New York City and want to call your uncle in San Francisco. At what time will you place the call from New York to reach him during his lunch hour?

   Ⓐ 1:30 P.M. Ⓑ 3:30 P.M. Ⓒ 10:30 A.M. Ⓓ 12:30 P.M.

Notes for Home: Your child learned to use a time zone map.
Home Activity: With your child, use this map to practice converting time to other time zones of the United States.

Name ______________________ Date __________ **Vocabulary Review**

Use with Chapter 14.

Vocabulary Review

Directions: Choose the vocabulary word from the box that best completes each sentence. Write the word on the line provided. Not all words will be used.

monk	convent	serf	guild
nun	missionary	knight	lady
monastery	monarch	chivalry	epidemic

1. A group of people united by a common interest is a ______________.
2. A ______________ served as a center of religion and education, as well as a community in which monks lived.
3. ______________ is another word for a disease that spreads quickly over a wide area.
4. A woman who devoted her life to religion in the Christian church was called a ______________.
5. Knights had a code of behavior called ______________.
6. A monk sometimes became a ______________ to teach his religion to people with different beliefs.

Directions: On the lines provided, write a short paragraph using at least three of the six words not used above. Use information from the chapter in your paragraph.

____

____

____

____

____

____

____

Notes for Home: Your child learned the vocabulary terms for Chapter 14.
Home Activity: Read aloud each word in the box. Ask your child to define each term.

Name ______________________ Date __________

UNIT 5 Project A Day in the Life

Use with Page 420.

Directions: In a group, make a documentary about living in a medieval village.

1. The ✔ shows the topics included in our documentary:

___location of village ___village buildings ___building materials

___surrounding landscape ___people in the village ___farming

___animals ___technology ___other activities

2. Facts to include in our script:

____

____

____

____

____

3. Parts of the village that we want to include in our model:

______________________ ______________________

______________________ ______________________

______________________ ______________________

✔ Checklist for Students

_____ We chose topics about life in a medieval village.
_____ We researched the topics.
_____ We wrote the script for our documentary.
_____ We built a model of a medieval village.
_____ We presented our documentary to the class.

Notes for Home: Your child learned about life in a medieval village.
Home Activity: With your child, make a Venn diagram to compare and contrast a medieval village to the city or town in which you live. Include information about location, buildings, people, and activities in your diagram.

Name ______________________ Date ______________ Reading Social Studies

Use with Pages 426–427.

Summarize

Directions: Read the following passage. Then fill in the circle next to the correct answer.

Leonardo da Vinci is considered one of the greatest painters, sculptors, architects, engineers, and scientists of the Renaissance period. He could paint, sculpt, sketch, and even design and build weapons, buildings, and machinery.

Da Vinci was interested in many things, but he rarely finished what he started. In fact, in a 17-year period, many art historians believe Da Vinci completed only six paintings, including *The Last Supper,* his masterpiece. He also painted the *Mona Lisa*, one of the world's most celebrated portraits.

Da Vinci produced theater designs, architectural designs, models, and statues. However, many were never finished or were lost or destroyed. He also made several scientific discoveries and even invented a large number of machines. Among them was an underwater diving suit and several flying devices.

1. Which of the following best summarizes the passage?

Ⓐ Da Vinci mainly was a painter.
Ⓑ Da Vinci's interests were so broad, he rarely finished a painting.
Ⓒ Da Vinci introduced approaches and styles to his art in an entirely new way.
Ⓓ Da Vinci was one of the greatest artists of the Renaissance period.

2. What is the main idea of the second paragraph?

Ⓐ Da Vinci completed only six paintings during his lifetime.
Ⓑ Because his interests were so broad, Da Vinci rarely finished works that he started.
Ⓒ *The Last Supper* is Da Vinci's masterpiece.
Ⓓ Da Vinci produced architectural designs and made scientific discoveries.

3. Which detail does NOT contribute to a summary of this passage?

Ⓐ Many of Da Vinci's works were lost or destroyed.
Ⓑ Da Vinci is recognized as one of the world's great Renaissance painters.
Ⓒ Da Vinci made several contributions to the arts and sciences.
Ⓓ Da Vinci's interests extended far beyond painting and sculpting.

Notes for Home: Your child learned how to summarize written passages.
Home Activity: Read a newspaper article, magazine article, or story with your child. Then ask your child to verbally summarize the passage.

Name ______________________ Date ____________

Vocabulary Preview

Directions: Use the vocabulary terms in the box to complete each sentence. Write the term on the lines. Then unscramble the letters marked with a star to answer the clue that follows.

commerce	excommunicate	conquistador	mercantilism
indulgence	circumnavigate	colony	

1. One of Magellan's ships was the first to _ _ _ _ _ _ _ _ _ _ _ _ _ _, or sail completely around, the world.

2. An economic system by which a country uses colonies to obtain raw materials is called _ _ _ _ _ _ _ _ _ _ _ _.

3. An _ _ _ _ _ _ _ _ _ _ is a church's pardon from punishment for a sin.

4. Hernando Cortés was a Spanish conqueror, or _ _ _ _ _ _ _ _ _ _ _ _, who acquired wealth by conquering a wealthy civilization.

5. The buying and selling of a large quantity of goods is called _ _ _ _ _ _ _ _.

6. A settlement physically separate from—but under the control of—the ruling country is a _ _ _ _ _ _.

7. Church officials could _ _ _ _ _ _ _ _ _ _ _ _ _, or expel, someone who challenged the church.

Clue: What is the name of the intellectual and economic movement that saw a revived interest in art and the social, scientific, and political thoughts of ancient Greece and Rome?

_ _ _ _ _ _ _ _ _ _ _ _

Notes for Home: Your child learned the vocabulary terms for Chapter 15.
Home Activity: With your child, review the above sentences. Then have your child give the definition for each vocabulary term.

Name ______________________ Date ____________ **Lesson Review**

Use with Pages 430–437.

Lesson 1: The Renaissance

Directions: Use complete sentences to answer the following questions on the lines provided. You may use your textbook.

1. Why did the Renaissance begin?

____

____

____

____

2. How was Renaissance art different from medieval European art?

____

____

____

____

Directions: Complete the chart with information about the Reformation and the Catholic Counter-Reformation. You may use your textbook.

	Reformation	Catholic Counter-Reformation
Why did the movement occur?		
What were followers' beliefs?		
What actions did followers take?		

Notes for Home: Your child learned about the changes in Europe brought on by the Renaissance.
Home Activity: With your child, discuss how events that occurred during the Renaissance affect us today.

Name ______________________ Date ____________ **Lesson Review**

Use with Pages 438–442.

Lesson 2: Trade Routes and Conquests

Directions: Match each name or term in the box to its description. Write the letter of the term on the line provided. You may use your textbook.

a. Portugal	**f.** Spain	**k.** Columbian Exchange
b. Ptolemy's map	**g.** Queen Isabella	**l.** Elizabeth I
c. Vasco da Gama	**h.** Pope Nicholas V	**m.** Armada
d. Ferdinand Magellan	**i.** Treaty of Tordesillas	
e. Christopher Columbus	**j.** Hernando Cortés	

____ **1.** conquistador who acquired wealth by conquering a wealthy civilization

____ **2.** queen of England; funded many expeditions and supported Dutch Protestants who were fighting against Catholic Spain

____ **3.** allowed explorers to make slaves of native peoples in newly explored lands

____ **4.** sailed around the Cape of Good Hope, which marked the first all-water trade route between Europe and Asia

____ **5.** agreement dividing the Americas between Spain and Portugal

____ **6.** sea captain whose ship was the first to sail completely around the world

____ **7.** world map used widely by navigators and sailors

____ **8.** fleet of Spanish warships defeated by English ships

____ **9.** funded Columbus's expedition to Asia; wanted to spread Christianity and compete with Portugal for wealth

____ **10.** important trading and naval power; took the lead in expeditions to find new sea routes

____ **11.** process of exchanging goods and diseases between the Americas and Europe

____ **12.** Italian sailor who sailed for Spain in search of a western route to Asia

____ **13.** Portugal's rival for wealth from voyages of exploration

Notes for Home: Your child learned about European expeditions, trade routes, and conquests.
Home Activity: With your child, imagine you are about to go on a voyage that will last several months. Make a list of the items and supplies you need to take with you. Discuss why each item is important.

Name ______________________ Date __________ **Lesson Review**

Use with Pages 444–449.

Lesson 3: European Colonization

Directions: Identify the European country associated with each of the following events. For Portugal write *P* in the blank, for Spain write *S*, for England write *E*, and for France write *F*. You may use your textbook.

___ **1.** a colony was formed in the region where Aztecs had been defeated

___ **2.** thirteen colonies had been established in North America by 1732

___ **3.** began exploring Africa in the early 1400s to spread Christianity

___ **4.** encomienda system of forced labor was established by government

___ **5.** colonization caught the interest of merchants and other people who sought wealth and religious and political freedom

___ **6.** clashes over land rights with Native Americans and British resulted in war in North America

___ **7.** first colony was settled by citizens who did not own land in home country

___ **8.** convicts were sent to settle New South Wales, Australia

___ **9.** landed in South America as early as 1500

___ **10.** control of Canada was lost after defeat by Great Britain

___ **11.** Mexico, Central America, part of South America, islands in the Caribbean, and the southwestern United States were controlled by 1550

___ **12.** Canada was claimed after explorations by Jacques Cartier

___ **13.** first colony was founded at Quebec

___ **14.** Brazil was first colony

___ **15.** first successful North American colony, Jamestown, was established

___ **16.** set up sugar cane plantations and forced Native Americans to work in Brazil

Notes for Home: Your child learned about early colonization by the Portuguese, Spanish, English, and French.
Home Activity: With your child, discuss how Europeans changed the ways of life of the native peoples in the lands they conquered and settled.

Name ______________________ Date __________

Use with Pages 450–451.

Interpret Political Cartoons

Political cartoons use humor and pictures to express the opinion or point of view of the cartoonist. This type of editorial usually focuses on public figures, political events, or economic conditions of a particular time and place. The cartoons often exaggerate events or personal qualities of the subject to make the cartoonist's point of view or message more obvious to the reader.

Directions: Read the questions about political cartoons. Fill in the circle next to the correct answer.

1. What is a political cartoon?

Ⓐ advertisement for a political figure
Ⓑ newspaper article written by a reporter
Ⓒ small caption that explains a photograph in a newspaper
Ⓓ interpretation of a current event through pictures and some words

2. Which of the following is NOT used in political cartoons to make a point?

Ⓐ drawings
Ⓑ captions
Ⓒ explanations
Ⓓ symbols

3. Which is NOT a reason why cartoonists use political cartoons to make a point?

Ⓐ Readers prefer straight text with no bias.
Ⓑ Cartoons are able to communicate meaning on several levels.
Ⓒ Their use of humor may soften a difficult or painful situation.
Ⓓ Readers often are more open to a visual message.

4. Which of the following activities may NOT help readers interpret political cartoons?

Ⓐ Study the relationships between the characters and symbols.
Ⓑ Identify any bias.
Ⓒ Determine the cartoonist's point of view on the topic.
Ⓓ Look for context clues in the articles surrounding the cartoon.

Directions: On a separate sheet of paper, draw a political cartoon about a newsworthy event.

Notes for Home: Your child learned to interpret political cartoons.
Home Activity: Using recent newspapers and magazines, help your child select a political cartoon to study. Discuss the cartoon's message and the cartoonist's point of view.

Name ______________________ Date __________ Vocabulary Review

Use with Chapter 15.

Vocabulary Review

Directions: Circle the vocabulary term that best completes each sentence. Then write the definition of that term on the line. You may use your textbook.

1. A practice of churches in western Europe that was most objected to was a willingness to accept money for a pardon, or (excommunicate, mercantilism, indulgence).

   ____

2. The Treaty of Tordesillas divided the Americas between Spain and Portugal and allowed a (colony, conquistador, commerce) to claim a portion of the Americas for either Spain or Portugal.

   ____

3. A (colony, circumnavigate, conquistador) helped make a ruling country wealthy and powerful by serving as a new market that could trade only with the ruling country.

   ____

   ____

4. The city-states of Florence, Milan, and Venice grew through trade and (commerce, mercantilism, indulgence).

   ____

5. Following Ferdinand Magellan's death, the last remaining ship in his voyage was the first to (conquistador, excommunicate, circumnavigate) the world.

   ____

6. The Europeans used an economic policy called (mercantilism, indulgence, colony) in their colonies to gain wealth and power.

   ____

   ____

7. When Martin Luther wrote a challenge to the Roman Catholic Church, church officials decided to (circumnavigate, indulgence, excommunicate) him from the church.

   ____

Notes for Home: Your child learned the vocabulary terms for Chapter 15.
Home Activity: With your child, make a set of vocabulary cards. Write the vocabulary words on one side. On the other side, write the definitions. Shuffle the cards and hold up each card, allowing your child to give you the matching word or definition.

Name ______________________ Date __________ **Vocabulary Preview**

Use with Chapter 16.

Vocabulary Preview

Directions: Match each vocabulary word in the box below with its meaning. Write the vocabulary word on the line next to its meaning.

legislature	textile	corporation
massacre	factory	reformer
monarchy	tenement	strike

1. ______________________ overcrowded slum apartment

2. ______________________ person who wanted to keep capitalism but improve it

3. ______________________ government in which a king, queen, or emperor has supreme power

4. ______________________ lawmaking body

5. ______________________ cloth that is either woven or knitted

6. ______________________ event that causes the death of unresisting or helpless people

7. ______________________ refusal to work until certain demands are granted

8. ______________________ large place where machines are grouped together

9. ______________________ business organization that raises money by selling stock shares to the public

Notes for Home: Your child learned the vocabulary terms for Chapter 16.
Home Activity: Call out each term and have your child use it in an original sentence.

Name ______________________ Date __________ **Lesson Review**

Use with Pages 456–462.

Lesson 1: Revolutions in the Americas

Directions: Complete the cause-and-effect chart with information from Lesson 1. You may use your textbook.

1. Cause Great Britain was deeply in debt.	→	**Effect**
2. Cause	→	**Effect** British government closed the port and sent troops to Boston.
3. Cause Great Britain sent over more troops to force the colonists to obey Parliament's laws.	→	**Effect**
4. Cause	→	**Effect** In 1783 the British accepted the United States as an independent nation.
5. Cause In 1791 Toussaint L'Ouverture led enslaved Africans in a revolt against French rule.	→	**Effect**
6. Cause	→	**Effect** His words set off a struggle for freedom in Mexico and Latin America.

Notes for Home: Your child learned how nations in the Americas were able to break free of European rule.
Home Activity: With your child, make a chart comparing and contrasting the ways citizens of these countries gained their independence.

Name ______________________ Date __________

Use with Pages 464–465.

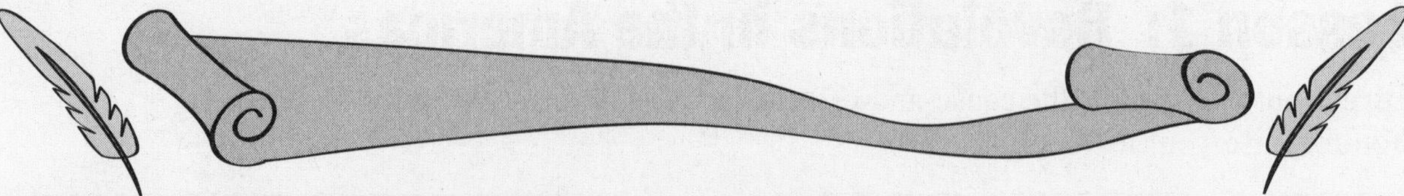

Writing Prompt: A New Nation

After the Revolutionary War was won, former colonists set about the task of creating a new nation. They wrote the U.S. Constitution to reflect the values of the citizens of the United States of America. Write a constitution for your school. What rights and liberties do you want to include?

____

____

____

____

____

____

____

____

____

____

____

____

____

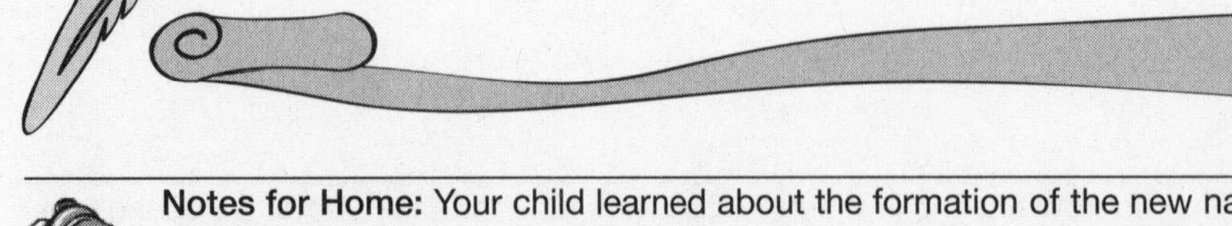

Notes for Home: Your child learned about the formation of the new nation.

Home Activity: With your child, discuss why it was important for the colonies to gain independence from Great Britain. Discuss how life today might be different if the United States had remained separate colonies under the rule of Great Britain.

Name ______________________ Date __________ **Lesson Review**

Use with Pages 466–470.

Lesson 2: The French Revolution

Directions: Sequence the events in the order in which they occurred. Number the events from 1 (earliest) to 12 (most recent). You may use your textbook.

_____ Radicals take control of the revolution and make France a republic.

_____ Members of the Third Estate form the National Assembly and write a constitution for France.

_____ King Louis XVI is put on trial as a traitor, convicted, and put to death.

_____ The French Revolution begins.

_____ Napoleon's armies conquer Spain, much of what is now Germany, and Austria.

_____ Fearing that the French Revolution might spread, other European rulers send armies into France, causing panic.

_____ During the Reign of Terror, thousands of citizens suspected of being against the revolution are put to death.

_____ The National Assembly adopts a *Declaration of the Rights of Man and of Citizen.*

_____ The Napoleonic Code preserves important reforms made by the republic during the French Revolution, but women lose some of the rights of citizenship they had gained.

_____ King Louis XVI calls a meeting of the Estates-General. The Third Estate demands that each person at the meeting have one vote, but the king refuses.

_____ Napoleon Bonaparte overthrows the French republic. He becomes emperor of France.

_____ Napoleon is defeated by Britain and European allies at the Battle of Waterloo.

Notes for Home: Your child learned about events occurring during the French Revolution.
Home Activity: With your child, discuss several events that have led to revolutions. Identify nonviolent means of bringing about change.

Name ______________________ Date __________ **Research and Writing Skills**

Use with Pages 472–473.

Compare Primary Sources

One way people learn about the past is by comparing primary sources, or the records of events made by people who witnessed them. In addition to written sources such as speeches, articles, and letters, primary sources include paintings, photographs, and artifacts.

Directions: In your textbook, locate and analyze the primary sources listed in the following chart. Then complete the chart to compare and contrast the sources.

Textbook Page	Primary Source	Information Provided in Primary Source	Draw Conclusions by Comparing Sources
p. 423	Quotation from King Ferdinand of Spain (1511)		How do the points of view in these quotations compare?
p. 427	Quotation from *In Defense of the Indians* by Bartolomé de Las Casas (1552)		
p. 111	Quotation from Ban Zhao, a female Chinese historian (some time around 100 B.C.)		How are these quotations alike and different?
p. 471	Quotation from *Declaration of the Rights of Woman and the Female Citizen* by Marie-Olympe De Gouges (1791)		

Notes for Home: Your child learned to compare primary sources.
Home Activity: Have your child think of a time when he or she had a disagreement or argument with someone. Together, compare your child's account of the argument to what might have been the other person's account. Discuss the similarities and differences in the two primary sources.

Name ______________________ Date ____________ **Lesson Review**

Use with Pages 474–477.

Lesson 3: The Industrial Revolution

In Europe after 1750, new ideas arose about how to make and use machines to produce goods faster and on a larger scale. This period is known as the Industrial Revolution.

Directions: Complete the chart with information about inventions or improvements made during the Industrial Revolution. You may use your textbook.

Invention	Inventor	Date	Purpose
Improvement of the Steam Engine			
Steamboat			
Train Engine			

Directions: Answer the following questions on the lines provided.

1. How and why did cities in Europe change during the Industrial Revolution?

____

____

____

____

2. What kinds of problems did Europe's growing cities experience?

Notes for Home: Your child learned about the beginning of the Industrial Revolution in Great Britain.
Home Activity: With your child, compare and contrast a typical day for a young British factory worker in the mid-1800s with a typical day in the life of your child.

Name ______________________ Date ____________ **Lesson Review**

Use with Pages 478–481.

Lesson 4: The Second Industrial Revolution

Directions: Write each term in the box beside its example or description.

Second Industrial Revolution	capitalism	labor union
internal combustion engine	market economy	socialism
electricity	*laissez faire*	Karl Marx
assembly line	reformer	

______________________ **1.** popularized socialist ideas and supported a classless society

______________________ **2.** organization formed to represent the workers in a factory or industry and demand higher wages and better working conditions

______________________ **3.** economic system in which private individuals own and run businesses for profit

______________________ **4.** run by oil made into gasoline

______________________ **5.** inventions that used electricity, oil, and steel for power and changed the way people lived and worked

______________________ **6.** manufacturing process in which individual workers add one part or perform one task to complete a product, such as an automobile

______________________ **7.** French expression meaning "leave it alone"; belief that government should not control business

______________________ **8.** supplied light and power to machines; led to new forms of communication

______________________ **9.** economic system in which the government owns most industries, businesses, land, and natural resources

______________________ **10.** person who wanted to keep capitalism but correct abuses in the system

______________________ **11.** economy in which people make their own decisions about how to spend their money

Notes for Home: Your child learned about the Second Industrial Revolution and the struggle to improve conditions for workers.
Home Activity: With your child, create a Venn diagram to compare and contrast capitalism and socialism. Discuss which form of government the United States has today.

Name ____________________ Date __________

Vocabulary Review

Use with Chapter 16.

Vocabulary Review

Directions: Read the following statements. Then write T (True) or F (False) on the line before each statement. If the answer is false, correct the statement to make it true. Not all words will be used. You may use your textbook.

___ **1.** A legislature is a lawmaking body that sets taxes and makes laws.

____

____

___ **2.** A reformer is a government in which a king, queen, or emperor has supreme power.

____

____

___ **3.** Workers bought raw materials such as cotton and produced thread to make tenements, or cloth that is either woven or knitted.

____

____

___ **4.** Businesspeople lowered costs by grouping machines together in one large factory.

____

____

___ **5.** In the cities, many workers lived in overcrowded slum apartments, called monarchies.

____

____

___ **6.** A strike is a refusal to work until certain demands are granted.

____

____

Notes for Home: Your child learned the vocabulary terms for Chapter 16.
Home Activity: With your child, scan the articles in a local newspaper. Locate as many of the vocabulary terms as you can and discuss how each term is used in the article.

Name ______________________ Date __________ **Vocabulary Preview**

Use with Chapter 17.

Vocabulary Preview

Directions: Find the meaning of each vocabulary term from Chapter 17. Write the meaning on the lines provided. You may use your textbook.

1. nationalism

____

____

2. imperialism

____

____

3. imperialist

____

4. treaty port

____

____

5. compound

____

6. modernization

____

____

7. dominion

____

____

8. parliament

____

____

Notes for Home: Your child learned the vocabulary terms for Chapter 17.
Home Activity: Use each term in an original sentence. Have your child restate the meaning of each vocabulary term in his or her own words.

Name ______________________ Date ____________ **Lesson Review**

Use with Pages 486–489.

Lesson 1: Expanding Empires

Directions: Circle the term that best completes each sentence.

1. (Nationalism, Imperialism, Colonization), or a strong devotion to one's own country, was a powerful force that swept over Europe in the 1800s.
2. Europeans made huge profits by selling factory-made goods created from raw materials obtained from their (enemies, allies, colonies).
3. In the age of imperialism, (Spain, Great Britain, China) had the largest empire in the world.
4. During the 1800s (India, Indochina, Egypt), was one of Great Britain's most valuable colonies.
5. Because many Indians were unhappy with British rule, called the (imperialism, reign, Raj), they rebelled.
6. The Indian National Congress, formed in 1885, began a movement toward (war, independence, destruction) for India.
7. Because the (Suez Canal, Raj, Indians) shortened the sea route from England to India, the British wanted to control it.
8. Imperialism was at its height in (China, Africa, Asia), where lands were claimed by the European powers.
9. After the Berlin Conference, the only two African countries remaining independent were (Egypt and Libya, Ethiopia and Angola, Ethiopia and Liberia).
10. King Leopold II of Belgium controlled the Congo and forced Africans living there to (leave the region, work for him, go to war).

Directions: Sequence the events below on the time line.

British buy Egypt's ownership of Suez Canal	Indian troops rebel against British
European powers partition Africa	French begin Suez Canal

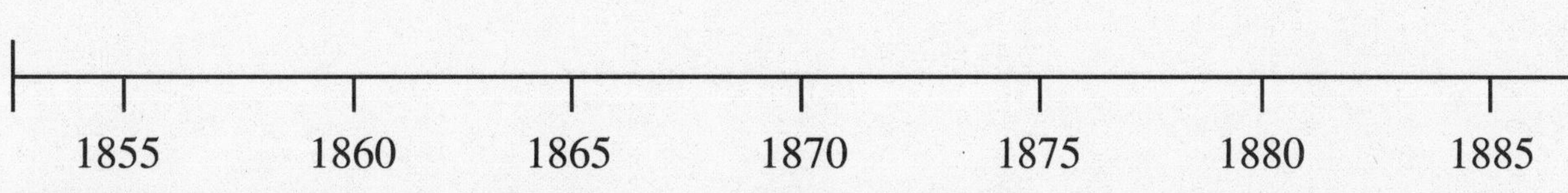

Notes for Home: Your child learned about European expansion in Africa in the 1800s.
Home Activity: With your child, review this lesson and make a list of the effects of imperialism on Africa.

Name ______________________ Date ____________ **Chart and Graph Skills**

Use with Pages 490–491.

Interpret Circle Graphs

Directions: Answer the following questions about circle graphs on the lines provided. You may use your textbook.

1. What information does a circle graph show?

____

____

____

2. How is information on a circle graph represented?

____

____

____

3. What percentage of a whole does an entire circle represent? Half a circle? A quarter of a circle?

____

____

____

4. How do you read a circle graph to analyze the information on it?

____

____

____

5. When might someone choose to show information on a circle graph rather than as a paragraph of text?

____

____

____

Notes for Home: Your child learned to interpret circle graphs.
Home Activity: With your child, identify how much time your child spends sleeping, at school, and on other activities in a typical day. Use this information to make a circle graph.

Name ______________________ Date ____________ **Lesson Review**

Use with Pages 492–496.

Lesson 2: Imperialism in East Asia

The actions of the European imperialists affected China and Japan differently.

Directions: Complete the chart by placing a (✔) in the correct column to identify where each event occurred. If the event occurred both in China and Japan, check the column labeled *Both*.

	China	Japan	Both
1. Qing dynasty powerless to keep out foreigners			
2. Lost much of its land to other countries			
3. Forced to open treaty ports			
4. Built up their armed forces and became more powerful			
5. Could not arrest Europeans			
6. Competed with Russia for control of Manchuria			
7. Fought in the first and second Opium Wars			
8. Began to be treated equally with Europeans			
9. Started on a path of modernization under new ruler			
10. Forced to open up country to trade			
11. "Boxers" wanted to destroy all foreign influences			
12. Attracted European imperialists			
13. Gained island of Formosa and won influence in Korea			
14. Went to war with Japan and was defeated			
15. Considered a great world power after defeating Russia			
16. Learned much about Western science and industry			

Notes for Home: Your child learned how imperialism affected China and Japan differently.
Home Activity: With your child, review information from the chapter and discuss what caused China to lose power while Japan became a world power. What might China have done differently to remain in control?

Name ______________________ Date __________ **Lesson Review**

Use with Pages 498–503.

Lesson 3: New Nations

Directions: Sequence the events leading to a united Italy in the order in which they took place. Number them from 1 (earliest) to 8 (most recent). You may use your textbook.

___ **1.** Southern Italy unites with the rest of the country; the kingdom of Italy is formally announced.

___ **2.** A movement for Italian unification builds.

___ **3.** Italy takes over Rome and makes it the Italian capital.

___ **4.** Giuseppe Garibaldi's army frees Sicily, Naples, and other parts of southern Italy.

___ **5.** Camillo di Cavour of the Kingdom of Sardinia forms an alliance with France; the allies attack Austria and drive the Austrians out of most of northern Italy.

___ **6.** Italy becomes a united nation.

___ **7.** Most states in northern and central Italy join with Sardinia under Victor Emmanuel II.

___ **8.** Italy takes over Venice and other nearby lands.

Directions: Match each dominion of the British Empire in the box to its description. Write the name of the dominion on the line. The terms will be used more than once.

Canada	Australia	New Zealand

______________ **9.** began when colonists and convicts settled in New South Wales

______________ **10.** included four provinces: Quebec, Ontario, New Brunswick, and Nova Scotia

______________ **11.** originally settled by Polynesian people called the Maori

______________ **12.** became a British dominion in 1907

______________ **13.** William Hobson signed treaty making this a British colony

______________ **14.** Sir Edmund Barton drew up constitution making this a British dominion in 1901

______________ **15.** became first British dominion in 1867

Notes for Home: Your child learned about new nations in Europe and the British colonies.
Home Activity: With your child, compare and contrast the German, Italian, and British nations. Why did they want to unify and build new nations? What changes did the governments make during the spread of nationalism?

Name ____________________ Date __________ **Vocabulary Review**

Use with Chapter 17.

Vocabulary Review

Directions: Circle the vocabulary term that best completes each sentence. You may use your textbook.

1. Because the British were pressured by some of their colonies for self-rule, they prepared each colony to become a (parliament, dominion, treaty port).

2. A European treaty port ran its own (dominion, parliament, compound), or enclosed area.

3. A powerful feeling called (parliament, nationalism, modernization) led some people to believe that their country was better than all others.

4. Meiji and his advisors started Japan on a path of rapid (parliament, nationalism, modernization), because Japan wanted to catch up with the West.

5. An elected legislature, or (parliament, compound, imperialist), enacts laws and selects national leaders from its own members.

6. A European who promoted building up an empire by controlling or conquering lands was called an (imperialism, dominion, imperialist).

7. A city such as Shanghai, where Europeans had special trading rights, was called a (treaty port, dominion, compound).

8. An idea often linked to the nationalism of the 1800s was (modernization, parliament, imperialism), which meant building up an empire by controlling or conquering lands in Africa, Asia, and elsewhere.

Directions: Answer the following question on the lines provided.

9. How did Japan use modernization to become a great world power?

____

____

____

____

Notes for Home: Your child learned the vocabulary terms for Chapter 17.
Home Activity: Write each vocabulary word on a small slip of paper. Then make a second set of papers on which you write the definitions. Have your child practice matching each term with its definition.

Name ______________________ Date ____________

Discovery Channel SCHOOL

Use with Page 510.

UNIT 6 Project Arts and Letters

Directions: In a group, advertise an important invention in an infomercial.

1. Our invention: ______________________

2. The ✔ shows the information included in our infomercial:

___invention name	___value (how it is helpful)
___inventor's name	___price
___description	___importance of invention
___how to use it	___other: ______________

3. Brief infomercial script (including facts about information above):

____

____

____

____

____

____

✔ Checklist for Students

_____ We chose an invention.

_____ We researched facts about the invention.

_____ We wrote a script for our infomercial.

_____ We made a poster to advertise the invention.

_____ We presented our infomercial to the class.

Notes for Home: Your child learned about important inventions.
Home Activity: With your child, look for items in your home that are important to people's daily lives. Discuss how life might be different if these items had never been invented or produced.

Cause and Effect

The European powers had several reasons for trying to expand their empires in the late 1800s.

Directions: Read p. 521 in your textbook. Then, for each of the following, fill in the circle next to the correct answer.

1. What caused intense competition among the nations of Europe during the late 1800s?

Ⓐ communism
Ⓑ nationalism
Ⓒ imperialism
Ⓓ nationalism and imperialism

2. What led some European nations to begin colonizing?

Ⓐ They had too many people and needed a place where peasants could live.
Ⓑ They did not like where they currently lived.
Ⓒ They wanted to claim new resources for their growing industries.
Ⓓ They were poor and needed money.

3. What did Germany do to make it easier to take and keep colonies?

Ⓐ became allies with Great Britain
Ⓑ became allies with France
Ⓒ paid foreign peoples to become German citizens
Ⓓ built a powerful navy

4. What caused many Africans and Asians to lose their independence during the nineteenth century?

Ⓐ famine
Ⓑ civil wars
Ⓒ colonization by Western European countries
Ⓓ disease

5. What led Great Britain and France to join forces against Germany in 1911?

Ⓐ Germany tried to seize a Moroccan port.
Ⓑ The Ottoman Empire was a target for colonization.
Ⓒ Germany added to its naval power.
Ⓓ They believed Germany already had too many colonies.

Notes for Home: Your child learned how the countries of Western Europe expanded their influence to other lands.
Home Activity: Discuss with your child how imperial expansion spreads the culture and influence of the colonizing nation to the nation being colonized. Brainstorm a list of ways your family's life might change if the United States were colonized by Great Britain, France, or Germany.

Name ______________________ Date ____________ **Vocabulary Preview**

Use with Chapter 18.

Vocabulary Preview

These are the vocabulary words for Chapter 18. How much do you know about these words?

Directions: Match each word with its meaning. Write the letter of the word on the line next to its meaning. You may use your glossary.

a. mobilization	___ preparations nations make before sending their armies into battle
b. neutral	___ payment for war losses
c. casualty	___ not taking sides
d. trench warfare	___ rapid increase in prices
e. armistice	___ mass killing
f. holocaust	___ a cease-fire agreement
g. reparation	___ wounded or killed soldier
h. inflation	___ armies dig deep ditches to shelter their troops

Directions: Write the vocabulary word that best completes each sentence.

1. When war broke out in 1914, the United States remained ____________ by not entering the war immediately.

2. The Armenian ____________ was the first of several mass killings in the twentieth century.

3. Germany's war-torn economy was largely the result of huge ____________ payments to the Allies.

4. During periods of ____________, money loses value.

Notes for Home: Your child learned the vocabulary terms for Chapter 18.
Home Activity: Help your child use each of the vocabulary words in an original sentence.

Name ______________________ Date __________ **Lesson Review**

Use with Pages 520–523.

Lesson 1: Headed Toward War

Directions: The following is a list of the European Powers. Separate them into the alliances they formed. Write *TA* if the country was a member of the Triple Alliance. Write *TE* if it was a member of the Triple Entente. Then answer the questions that follow. You may use your textbook.

____ **1.** Great Britain

____ **2.** Italy

____ **3.** France

____ **4.** Germany

____ **5.** Austria-Hungary

____ **6.** Russia

7. What effect did these alliances have on the possibility of war?

____

____

____

____

8. Name one advantage and one disadvantage of a country being part of a large alliance.

____

____

____

____

Notes for Home: Your child learned about the alliances formed by the European Powers before the Great War.
Home Activity: With your child, discuss the similarities and differences between a friendship and a formal alliance.

Name ______________________ Date __________

Chart and Graph Skills

Use with Pages 524-525.

Compare Parallel Time Lines

Directions: Use the information in the parallel time lines to answer the following questions.

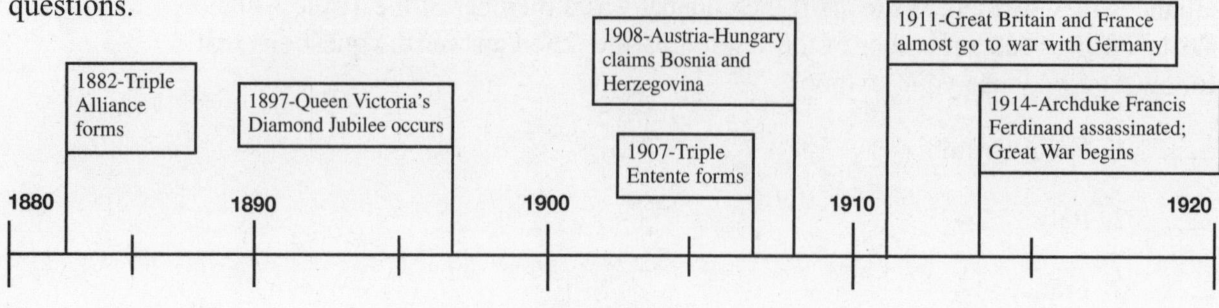

Europe

Ingrid

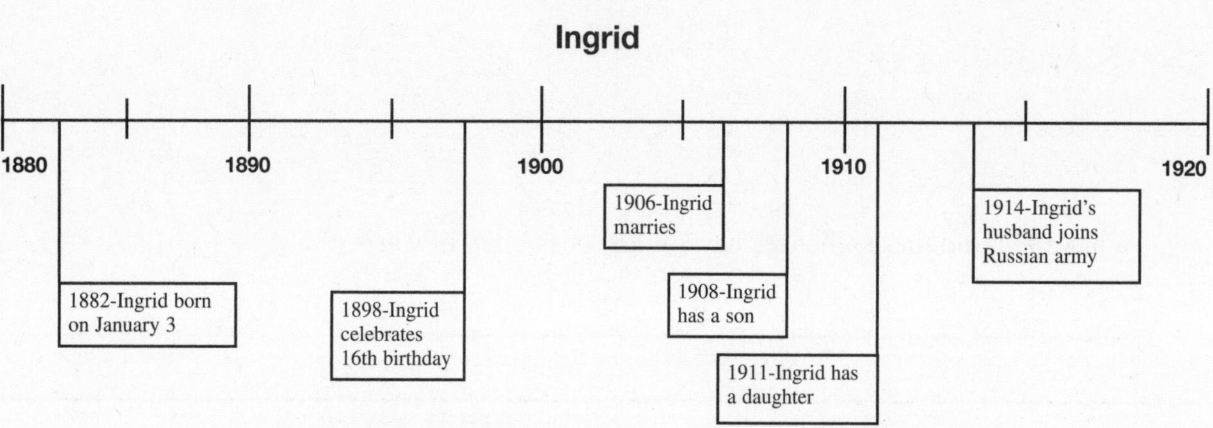

1. How old was Ingrid at the time of Queen Victoria's Diamond Jubilee?

____

2. What important world event occurred the year after Ingrid married?

____

3. What world event may have contributed to Ingrid's husband's decision to join the Russian army?

____

4. What event happened in Ingrid's family the year Austria-Hungary claimed Bosnia and Herzegovina?

____

Notes for Home: Your child learned how to analyze relationships between parallel time lines.
Home Activity: With your child, create a time line of activities and events from your child's life over the past week or month. Then create a parallel time line of U.S. or world events.

Name ______________________ Date ____________ **Lesson Review**

Use with Pages 526–532.

Lesson 2: The Great War

Directions: The Great War in Europe was fought along two fronts. Each of the following phrases deals with either the Eastern Front, the Western Front, or both. Place the number of each phrase under the appropriate heading in the Venn diagram below. You may use your textbook.

1. German, French, and British soldiers come to a standstill.

2. Russia battles Germany and Austria-Hungary.

3. Soldiers use new weapons such as poisonous gas, machine guns, and tanks.

4. For the first time, airplanes are used to drop bombs on the enemy.

5. Germans attack Verdun.

6. Thousands of soldiers die.

7. Allies storm German trenches.

8. Russian army suffers terrible casualties.

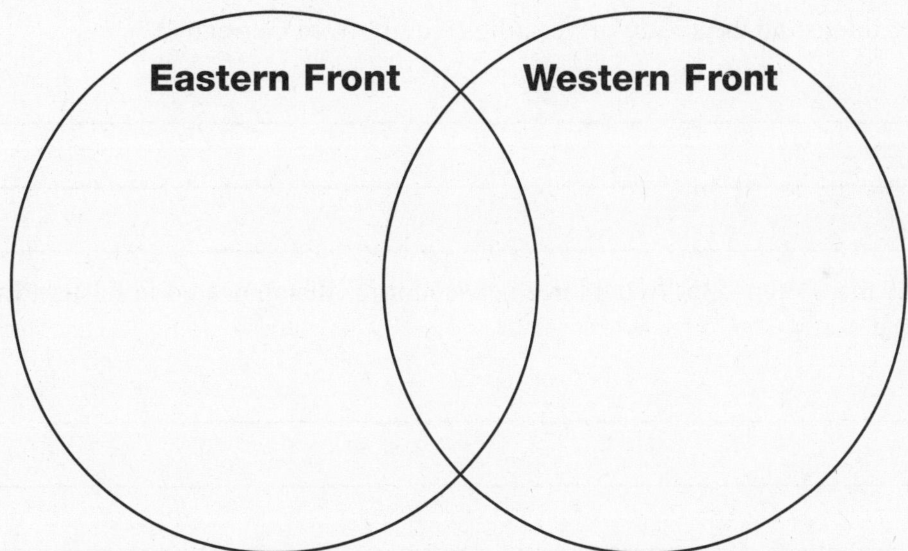

Notes for Home: Your child learned about the fighting in Europe during the Great War.
Home Activity: With your child, examine the map on p. 531. Discuss how people probably were affected when the war front moved into their home area.

Name ______________________ Date __________ **Lesson Review**

Use with Pages 534–537.

Lesson 3: After the War

The Great War caused events to follow in its aftermath.

Directions: Draw a line from each country in the first column to the corresponding phrase in the second column. Then answer the questions that follow.

1. Ottoman Empire	**a.** its President created Fourteen Points
2. United States	**b.** site of Armenian Holocaust
3. Russia (Soviet Union)	**c.** its money became virtually worthless
4. Germany	**d.** suffered the greatest number of casualties

5. What organization was formed from President Wilson's plan for a "general association of nations"?

____

____

____

6. What three things did the Treaty of Versailles require from Germany?

____

____

____

7. Look at the maps on p. 535. Name three new countries that appeared in Eastern Europe after the war.

____

____

____

Notes for Home: Your child learned about the results of the Great War.
Home Activity: Discuss with your child the provisions of the Treaty of Versailles. Ask him or her why the Allies might want to punish Germany in this way.

Name ______________________ Date __________ **Vocabulary Review**

Use with Chapter 18.

Vocabulary Review

Directions: Complete each sentence with the correct word or phrase.

mobilization	casualty	armistice	reparation
neutral	trench warfare	holocaust	inflation

1. In 1918 the Great War ended with an ______________.
2. Many families suffered at least one ______________ due to the fighting in the Great War.
3. The Germans were bound by the Treaty of Versailles to make ______________ payments to the Allies.
4. In Germany, ______________ made money so worthless that many people burned it for heat.
5. Some countries did not take sides in the war. They chose to remain ______________.
6. Europeans started the process of ______________ to prepare their armies for war.
7. Ottoman officials massacred between one-half million and one million Armenians in the first ______________ of the twentieth century.
8. When engaging in ______________, soldiers had to crawl out to fight the enemy.

Directions: On the lines below, use as many words as possible from the box above to write an imaginary news bulletin about the end of the Great War.

____

____

____

____

Notes for Home: Your child learned the vocabulary terms for Chapter 18.
Home Activity: Provide your child with one-word clues for each vocabulary term. Have him or her try to answer with the correct term while using as few clues as possible.

Name ______________________ Date ____________ **Vocabulary Preview**

Use with Chapter 19.

Vocabulary Preview

These are the vocabulary words for Chapter 19. How much do you know about these words?

Directions: Match each vocabulary word to its meaning. Write the number of the word on the line next to its meaning. You may use your glossary.

1. depression
2. fascism
3. Nazi
4. propaganda
5. aggression
6. annex
7. appeasement
8. collective
9. Axis Powers
10. Allies
11. Big Three
12. Women's Army Corps
13. D-Day
14. kamikaze
15. refugee
16. concentration camp
17. charter

_____ constitution

_____ Great Britain, Soviet Union, China, and the United States

_____ Germany's fascist party, the National Socialists

_____ a period of economic decline

_____ preserving peace by meeting the demands of an aggressor

_____ Germany, Italy, and Japan

_____ launching attacks on other countries

_____ armed forces organization for women

_____ to attach

_____ a person who left his or her homeland for safety

_____ June 6, 1944: history's largest invasion by sea

_____ the planned spread of certain beliefs using posters, pamphlets, and speeches

_____ a place that imprisoned people of a particular ethnic group or for their political or religious beliefs

_____ Franklin Roosevelt, Joseph Stalin, and Winston Churchill

_____ form of government that stresses the nation above individuals

_____ farms grouped together and run by the government

_____ Japanese pilots who flew their airplanes directly into enemy warships

Notes for Home: Your child learned the vocabulary terms for Chapter 19.
Home Activity: Explain to your child that these World War II terms still are used today. Together, use each term in a modern context.

Name ______________________ Date __________ **Lesson Review**

Use with Pages 542–547.

Lesson 1: Good to Bad Times

Directions: Think about what the following terms and names mean and how they relate to World War II. Then write them in the correct column in the chart. You may use your textbook.

Leaders	**Events**
Joseph Stalin	responsible for Kristallnacht
Emperor Hirohito	launched the Five-Year Plans
Adolf Hitler	became dictator of Italy
Benito Mussolini	took Manchuria

Country	Leader	Event
Italy		
Germany		
Japan		
Soviet Union		

Notes for Home: Your child learned about events leading to World War II.
Home Activity: With your child, review the chart. Discuss how all of these events were related during World War II.

Name ______________________ Date __________ **Lesson Review**

Use with Pages 548–554.

Lesson 2: World War II

Directions: Read the following events from World War II. Put them in the order that they occurred by numbering them from 1 (earliest) to 10 (latest). You may use your textbook.

___ **1.** The United States and France drive Germany out of Paris.

___ **2.** Japan surrenders.

___ **3.** Nazi Germany surrenders.

___ **4.** Germany attacks Poland.

___ **5.** German troops surrender to the Soviet Army at Stalingrad.

___ **6.** President Roosevelt dies.

___ **7.** D-Day occurs at Normandy.

___ **8.** Great Britain wins the battle at El Alamein.

___ **9.** The United States drops an atomic bomb on Hiroshima.

___ **10.** Japan attacks Pearl Harbor.

Directions: Answer the questions below. Write your answers on the lines provided.

1. What were some important contributions women in the United States made during World War II?

____

____

____

2. What might have happened if Japan had not ignored the United States warning about the atomic bomb?

____

____

Notes for Home: Your child learned about the sequence of events during World War II.
Home Activity: With your child, analyze the events in this worksheet to find cause-and-effect relationships.

Name ______________________ Date ____________

Use with Pages 556–557.

Writing Prompt: Victory!

The unconditional surrender of German forces in World War II took place on May 7, 1945. People commemorated the end of the war in Europe in many ways. Write a paragraph describing ways that people celebrated after the war was won. How did these celebrations represent the way people felt?

Notes for Home: Your child learned about the end of World War II.
Home Activity: With your child, discuss why it is important that the Allies—Britain, France, the United States, and the USSR—won World War II. Discuss how life today might be different if the United States and its allies had lost the war.

Name ____________________ Date __________

Lesson Review

Use with Pages 558–561.

Lesson 3: The Aftermath

Directions: Complete each sentence with the correct term from the box. You may use your textbook.

Joseph Stalin	Eleanor Roosevelt	Anne Frank
United Nations	Meyer Levin	Marshall Plan
6 million	13 billion	100,000

1. The atomic bomb left more than ____________________ dead and thousands more severely burned or sick with illnesses such as cancer.

2. Nazi Germany's "Final Solution" left at least ____________________ Jewish people dead.

3. American reporter ____________________ described the horrors of the Nazi concentration camps.

4. The ____________________ was formed as an international peacekeeping organization.

5. The first U.S. delegate to the United Nations was ____________________.

6. After the war, aid was sent to Europe under the provisions of the

____________________.

7. The United States sent ____________________ dollars in aid to help rebuild European economies.

8. ____________________ forced Eastern European countries to refuse money from the United States after the war.

9. ____________________ expressed personal feelings about the war in a diary.

Notes for Home: Your child learned about events that occurred immediately after World War II.
Home Activity: With your child, discuss the actions of the Axis Powers and the consequences they suffered after the war. Then ask whether he or she thinks the Allies should have helped the Axis countries rebuild. Discuss the reasons behind Allied aid.

Name ______________________ Date __________ **Chart and Graph Skills**

Use with Pages 562–563.

Interpret Bar Graphs

Bar graphs help us understand relationships among amounts or numbers.

Directions: Look at the bar graphs and text on pages 562–563 of your textbook. Then read each statement below. On the line beside each statement, write a *T* if it is true. If it is false, write an *F* and then rewrite the false portion of the statement on the line provided to make it true.

___ **1.** Bar graphs have one axis.

____

___ **2.** The vertical axis on a graph is the y-axis.

____

___ **3.** On the graphs on pages 562–563, country names label the y-axis.

____

___ **4.** The heights of the bars indicate exact figures.

____

___ **5.** The title and axes labels on a graph help you read the information on the graph.

____

___ **6.** Italy had the fewest military casualties of all the countries represented on the graph.

____

___ **7.** On the graph, Japan spent the lowest percentage of its national income on defense.

____

Notes for Home: Your child learned to interpret a bar graph.
Home Activity: Using temperature data from a newspaper or weather broadcast, have your child create bar graphs to represent the high and low temperatures for five U.S. cities on today's date. Then quiz your child on the information recorded on the graphs.

Name ______________________ Date __________ **Vocabulary Review**

Use with Chapter 19.

Vocabulary Review

These are the vocabulary words for Chapter 19. How much do you know about these words?

Directions: Circle the word that best completes each sentence.

depression	annex	Big Three	concentration camp
fascism	appeasement	Women's Army Corps	charter
Nazi	collective	D-Day	
propaganda	Axis Powers	kamikaze	
aggression	Allies	refugee	

1. The (Nazis, charter) took away many democratic freedoms in Germany.
2. Because of the (depression, aggression), people around the world lacked hope.
3. In the political system called (appeasement, fascism) the leader has total control over the government and industry.
4. The Nazis spread new ideas rapidly through the use of (aggression, propaganda).
5. Hitler's and Mussolini's policies of (depression, aggression) helped lead to the outbreak of war.
6. Under Stalin's rule, Russian farmers worked on the land of a (collective, fascist) every day.
7. By 1942, the United States had joined the war on the side of the (Axis Powers, Allies).
8. Hitler decided to (annex, charter) Austria to gain more land.
9. The World War II Allies created a (charter, propaganda) to guide the actions of the United Nations.
10. An (appeasement, charter) means that peace can be preserved by meeting the demands of an aggressor.
11. Europe, China, and other areas were overflowing with (Nazis, refugees) as a result of the atomic bomb.
12. The Nazis forced many Jewish people into (charters, concentration camps).
13. Germany, Italy, and Japan made up the group known as the (Axis Powers, Allies).

Notes for Home: Your child learned the vocabulary terms for Chapter 19.
Home Activity: Write each of the vocabulary words on an index card and then shuffle the cards. Have your child draw a card from the stack and tell you one name, place, or event associated with that term in World War II. Continue until all the cards have been chosen.

Name ______________________ Date __________ **Vocabulary Preview**

Use with Chapter 20.

Vocabulary Preview

These are the vocabulary words from Chapter 20. How much do you know about these words?

Directions: Draw a line from the word to the correct definition.

1. nuclear	**a.** relaxation of tensions
2. containment	**b.** a hit-and-run-fighter
3. proletarian	**c.** atomic
4. guerilla	**d.** preventing the spread of communism
5. détente	**e.** "of the working class"

Directions: Suppose you are a newspaper reporter covering an international political crisis. Use the vocabulary words above to write a front-page story for your paper.

____

____

____

____

____

____

____

____

____

____

____

____

Notes for Home: Your child learned the vocabulary terms for Chapter 20.
Home Activity: These terms are all related to past political conflicts. With your child, read a newspaper article on current international disputes. Discuss how the conflict involves, or might lead to, the use of the terms shown above.

Name ______________________ Date ____________ **Lesson Review**

Use with Pages 568–572.

Lesson 1: The Soviets Advance

Directions: During the Cold War, tensions escalated between the United States and the Soviet Union. For every action one superpower took, the other nation responded. Read each action. Complete the table by identifying who took action, who reacted, and what the response was. You may use your textbook.

Action	By	Reaction	By
1. Stopped traffic into Berlin			
2. Set up NATO			
3. Tested first H-bomb			
4. Began building missile bases in Cuba			

Notes for Home: Your child learned that actions by one superpower caused a reaction by another.
Home Activity: Discuss major events at home or at work that caused reactions by other parties to those events. Review the cause-and-effect sequence of the actions.

Name ______________________ Date __________ **Thinking Skills**

Use with Pages 574–575.

Solve Complex Problems

The race to develop and stockpile nuclear arms is one in which superpowers and smaller countries alike participate. Some people view this arms race as an advantage for their country. Others consider any race that could threaten entire nations with complete destruction to be a disadvantage.

Directions: Complete the following problem-solving chart with details to support your views on the nuclear arms race.

Problem-Solving Process	
1. Identify a problem.	Should countries develop and stockpile nuclear arms?
2. Gather information.	
3. List and consider options.	
4. Consider advantages and disadvantages.	
5. Choose and implement a decision.	
6. Evaluate the effectiveness of a solution.	

Notes for Home: Your child learned to use a problem-solving process to solve complex problems.
Home Activity: Identify a complex issue with your child. Together, apply the steps in the problem-solving process to find a solution.

Name ______________________ Date ____________ **Lesson Review**

Use with Pages 576–580.

Lesson 2: Communism in China

After the removal of China's emperor in 1911, China went through changes in its government.

Directions: Use the phrases in the box to compare the Nationalist and Communist Parties. Then complete the Venn diagram with these phrases. You may use your textbook.

Tried to turn farms into collectives	Leader was Mao Zedong
Fought in a civil war	Started the Cultural Revolution
Kept seat in United Nations until 1971	Capital was Taipei
Invited to take UN seat in 1971	Fought Japan during World War II
Capital was Beijing	Leader was Chiang Kai-shek

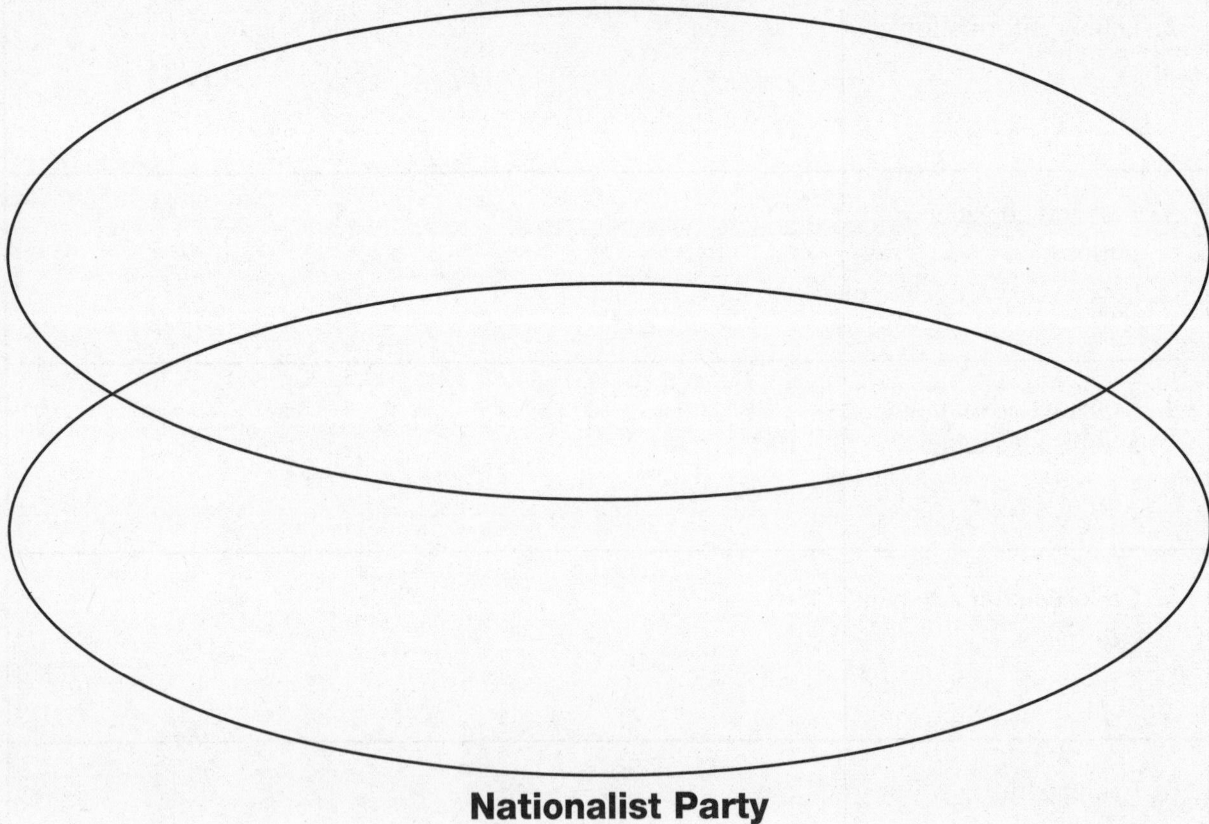

Notes for Home: Your child learned how leaders influenced the social and political direction of a country.
Home Activity: Discuss with your child the qualities effective leaders possess.

Name ______________________ Date ____________ **Lesson Review**

Use with Pages 582–587.

Lesson 3: The Cold War Heats Up

After World War II, the United States was involved in two wars in Asia. One war was fought in Korea, the other in Vietnam.

Directions: Read the following statements and decide which country is described. On the line beside each number, write a *K* for Korea or a *V* for Vietnam. Then answer the questions below. You may use your textbook.

____ **1.** An invasion was launched on June 25, 1950.

____ **2.** President Eisenhower promised help.

____ **3.** A demonstration against the war brought protesters to Washington, D.C.

____ **4.** The Tet offensive proved devastating to U.S. troops.

____ **5.** General MacArthur was put in charge of American troops.

____ **6.** Television brought the war to American homes.

____ **7.** China came to the aid of communist forces.

____ **8.** The war continued until April 1975.

____ **9.** President Truman requested action from the United Nations.

____ **10.** An armistice in 1953 ended the fighting.

1. Why did General MacArthur and President Truman disagree about how to fight in the Korean War?

____

____

____

2. Why did President Johnson think the United States had to fight in the war in Vietnam?

____

____

____

Notes for Home: Your child learned about the United States' participation in wars in Korea and Vietnam.
Home Activity: Share with your child any recollections you or other family members may have of either conflict. Discuss reasons for your support for or protest of American involvement in these wars.

Name ______________________ Date __________ **Vocabulary Review**

Use with Chapter 20.

Vocabulary Review

Directions: Complete each sentence with the correct vocabulary word from the box below.

nuclear	containment	proletarian	guerilla	détente

1. Unlike Korea, North Vietnam used ____________ fighters to attack its enemies.
2. President Truman used a policy of ____________ against communism.
3. Tensions between the Soviet Union and the United States during the Cold War escalated after the invention of ____________ weapons.
4. As the war in Vietnam came to an end, President Nixon enacted a plan of ____________.
5. Mao Zedong started a new phase of revolution in China called the "Great ____________ Cultural Revolution."

Directions: Use the vocabulary words from this chapter to create a fictional journal entry for Henry Kissinger. Explain the armistice between the United States and North Vietnam.

____

____

____

____

____

____

____

____

Notes for Home: Your child learned the vocabulary terms for Chapter 20.
Home Activity: Discuss the importance of maintaining peace among world powers that are involved in ongoing political conflicts.

Name ______________________ Date __________

Discovery Channel SCHOOL

UNIT 7 Project We Interrupt This Program

Use with Page 596.

Directions: In a group, present a news conference about a historic event in Unit 7.

1. The historic event chosen: ______________________.

2. Roles assigned for the news conference:

______ news anchor(s) ______ reporter(s)

______ government official(s) ______ citizen(s)

3. Press release (summary of the event):

Who: ______________________

What: ______________________

Where: ______________________

When: ______________________

Why: ______________________

How: ______________________

On a separate sheet of paper, write a summary of the event's importance in history.

✔ Checklist for Students

_____ We chose a historic event.

_____ We assigned roles for the news conference.

_____ We wrote a press release.

_____ We made a banner or brought materials to help describe the event.

_____ We presented our news conference to the class.

Notes for Home: Your child learned how to write a press release about an important event.
Home Activity: With your child, watch a local or national news program or news conference. Discuss how important events are summarized. Share details about the events and their importance to the world.

Name ______________________ Date ______________ **Reading Social Studies**

Use with Pages 602–603.

Draw Conclusions

Directions: Read the passage. Then answer the questions that follow.

From 1898 to 1997 Hong Kong, on the southeastern coast of China, was a British colony. For more than 150 years Hong Kong had been the financial center of Asia and the busiest shipping port in the world. Many people predicted this would change once Great Britain turned over Hong Kong to China.

Under British control, Hong Kong handled its own international trade. As part of the handover negotiations, China agreed not to interfere with Hong Kong's economy or democratic form of government for at least 50 years.

Although their economic and government systems are different, China and Hong Kong are in many ways interdependent. When Great Britain took control of Hong Kong, the population was mostly Chinese. Because the British did not force their own culture upon the colony, Chinese culture remained an important influence on the people of Hong Kong. Their shared customs and heritage have created a strong cultural bond between them, and the people of Hong Kong feel a certain loyalty to China.

Hong Kong serves as a major port for the Pacific region, including China. Its absence of import tariffs also makes it an important export market for goods from China. Hong Kong's free market system serves as a model for China, which is trying to modernize its economy and government.

Interaction with China is also important for Hong Kong to meet the basic needs of its people. Hong Kong depends on China for nearly 50 percent of its food and almost half of its water.

1. Which of the following statements is a logical conclusion for this passage?
   - Ⓐ Hong Kong's economy would benefit from a communist government.
   - Ⓑ The relationship between Hong Kong and China benefits both of them.
   - Ⓒ British colonization had no effect on the economy of Hong Kong.
   - Ⓓ Hong Kong would benefit from cutting its ties to China.

2. What conclusion can you draw from the passage about the future relationship between Hong Kong and China?
   - Ⓐ Citizens of Hong Kong will petition for a return to British rule.
   - Ⓑ China will no longer depend on Hong Kong ports for exporting its goods to overseas markets.
   - Ⓒ Hong Kong will agree to abide by a communist government.
   - Ⓓ As China and Hong Kong become more interdependent, they will continue to influence each other economically.

Notes for Home: Your child learned how to draw conclusions from printed text.
Home Activity: State four related details or facts about a topic of your choice. Have your child practice drawing a conclusion from the clues in your facts.

Name ______________________ Date __________

Vocabulary Preview

Use with Chapter 21.

Vocabulary Preview

Directions: Read each sentence in the box. Match the underlined word in each sentence with its synonym or definition below. Write the underlined term on the line next to its definition. You may use your glossary.

- The decolonization of Kenya was complete on December 12, 1963.
- In 1965 Mobutu took control of the Congo in a coup d'état.
- The Afrikaner party passed laws to segregate whites from blacks in South Africa.
- Nelson Mandela was imprisoned for protesting against South Africa's laws of apartheid.
- In the 1980s, many countries placed a sanction on South Africa to force the government to do away with apartheid.
- Gandhi's method of civil disobedience attracted many followers in India.
- The movement to build a Jewish state in Palestine became known as Zionism.
- Vaclav Havel, a former dissident, became president of Czechoslovakia.
- When Mikhail Gorbachev became the Communist Party leader, he introduced *perestroika* to reform the Soviet economy.
- *Glasnost* was a policy that gave Soviet people some freedom of speech.

______________ **1.** protester against the government

______________ **2.** system of laws enforcing segregation

______________ **3.** overthrow of the government

______________ **4.** refusal to obey or cooperate with unjust laws

______________ **5.** process of removing control by another country

______________ **6.** separate

______________ **7.** penalty

______________ **8.** policy that allowed Soviet people some freedom of speech

______________ **9.** policy introduced to reform the Soviet economy

______________ **10.** establishment of a Jewish state in Palestine

Notes for Home: Your child learned the vocabulary terms for Chapter 21.
Home Activity: Ask your child to use the terms from this chapter to explain to you the effects of decolonization in Africa, Asia, the Middle East, and Eastern Europe.

Name ______________________ Date ____________ **Lesson Review**

Use with Pages 606–612.

Lesson 1: Independence

Directions: Answer the following questions about the decolonization of Africa and Asia on the lines provided. You may use your textbook.

1. Why was decolonization important to the people of Africa and Asia?

____

____

2. What challenges did some new sub-Saharan African nations face after decolonization?

____

____

3. How did Western nations react to apartheid as a result of the protest in the town of Soweto?

____

____

____

4. What happened in South Africa as a result of Nelson Mandela's election as president?

____

____

5. What did Mohandas Gandhi urge people to do when he became the leader of India's independence movement?

____

____

____

6. How did religion influence the formation of Pakistan?

____

____

Notes for Home: Your child learned how nations in Africa and Asia gained independence from European rule.
Home Activity: With your child, discuss the advantages and disadvantages of independence for any nation.

Name ____________________ Date __________ **Lesson Review**

Use with Pages 614–618.

Lesson 2: The Middle East

Directions: Match each cause with its effect. Write the letter of the effect on the line provided after each cause. You may use your textbook.

Cause

1. Jews face anti-Semitism in Europe. ____
2. Jews are persecuted in Nazi Germany. ____
3. A conflict grows between Arabs and Jews. ____
4. Arab states refuse to recognize the state of Israel. ____
5. Israel reaches an armistice with its Arab neighbors. ____
6. A coup d'état ends the monarchy in Egypt. ____
7. Nasser goes to war against France, Great Britain, and Israel. ____
8. Israel and its Arab neighbors fight the Six-Day War. ____
9. Arab states attack Israel and place an embargo on oil exports to Western countries supporting Israel. ____
10. Anwar el-Sadat becomes president of Egypt. ____

Effect

a. Israel gains a large portion of the land that was to become an Arab state.

b. Leaders in the Middle East attempt to make peace.

c. Arab nationalism becomes a powerful force in the Middle East.

d. Many Jews leave Europe for Palestine and the United States.

e. Israel controls Palestine, the Gaza Strip, the West Bank, the Golan Heights, and the Sinai Peninsula.

f. The United Nations proposes dividing Palestine into an Arab state and a Jewish state.

g. Gamal Abdel Nasser becomes the prime minister of Egypt.

h. War breaks out between Arabs and Jews.

i. The largest migration of Jews to Palestine takes place.

j. An international oil crisis occurs.

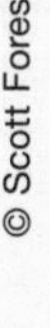

Notes for Home: Your child learned about conflicts in the Middle East between Arabs and Jews.
Home Activity: With your child, discuss the importance of finding nonviolent ways to solve disagreements. Have your child give examples of efforts to create peace in the Middle East.

Name ______________________ Date __________ **Lesson Review**

Use with Pages 620–623.

Lesson 3: Eastern Europe

Directions: Sequence the events in the order in which they took place by numbering them from 1 (earliest) to 13 (most recent). You may use your textbook.

____ Mikhail Gorbachev calls for more freedoms for Soviet people.

____ The people of Hungary rebel against their communist government.

____ Boris Yeltsin and other leaders of the republics declare the end of the Soviet Union in December 1991.

____ The destruction of the Berlin Wall is complete.

____ Yeltsin begins to change the Russian economy and 15 new nations are created.

____ People in East Germany protest against their communist government.

____ East Germany and West Germany are reunited into one country.

____ Workers in Poland led by Lech Walesa force their government to accept Solidarity.

____ The people of Czechoslovakia want freedom, but their demands are rejected by the Soviet Union.

____ After World War II, the Soviet Union forces communist governments on countries in Eastern Europe.

____ Poland holds free elections in 1989.

____ Russia becomes a communist country.

____ Mikhail Gorbachev resigns as president of the Soviet Union.

Notes for Home: Your child learned about the end of communism in Eastern Europe and the Soviet Union.
Home Activity: With your child, discuss the freedoms citizens might lose in a communist country. Discuss why citizens of the former Soviet Union might want more personal freedoms.

Name ______________________ Date __________ **Thinking Skills**

Use with Pages 624–625.

Determine Accuracy of Information

When gathering information, it is important to use source material that is accurate and credible. Outdated information can provide old statistics and lead to false conclusions. An author who projects bias or is not a credible source for a topic can state opinions as facts, which can mislead the reader.

Directions: Fill in the circle next to the correct answer.

1. Which of the following online sources would be most likely to post unbiased information about a recent world crisis?

Ⓐ government Web site
Ⓑ online chat room
Ⓒ family home page
Ⓓ e-mail from an eyewitness

2. Which of the following print sources would be most likely to provide a firsthand account of the fall of the Berlin Wall?

Ⓐ novel about the reunification of Germany
Ⓑ article from a recent monthly German teen magazine
Ⓒ diary entry from an eyewitness to the event
Ⓓ entry in a world almanac

3. Which of the following print sources would be most likely to provide reliable statistics on the population of your state?

Ⓐ publication of the U.S. Census Bureau
Ⓑ 1990 almanac
Ⓒ encyclopedia
Ⓓ geographic dictionary

4. Which of the following would be most likely an objective source for a report on the decolonization of India?

Ⓐ speech by Mohandas Gandhi
Ⓑ declaration by the British government
Ⓒ biography of Jawaharlal Nehru
Ⓓ encyclopedia entry on the history of India in the twentieth century

Notes for Home: Your child learned how to analyze sources for accuracy of information.
Home Activity: With your child, read two accounts of the same event from different sources. Then compare the sources for accuracy, currentness, and objectivity.

Name ______________________ Date __________

Use with Chapter 21.

Vocabulary Review

Directions: Imagine you were present for one of the events in the chapter. Use the terms in the box to write a firsthand account about the event. Use the diary page below to write your paragraphs.

decolonization	apartheid	dissident
coup d'état	sanction	perestroika
segregate	civil disobedience	glasnost
	Zionism	

Notes for Home: Your child learned the vocabulary words for Chapter 21.
Home Activity: Have your child use each word in context. Together, use the words to discuss more recent world events.

Name ______________________ Date __________ **Vocabulary Preview**

Use with Chapter 22.

Vocabulary Preview

Directions: Match each vocabulary word in the box to its meaning. Write the vocabulary word on the line before the definition. You may use your glossary.

gross domestic product	trade agreement	ethnic cleansing
trading bloc	ethnicity	repressive
euro	multiethnic nation	terrorism

______________________ **1.** policy of driving out or killing people who do not share the same identity

______________________ **2.** sharing the same language, customs, and other aspects of culture

______________________ **3.** understanding that outlines rules about the exchange of goods between countries

______________________ **4.** group of countries that agree to trade under favorable conditions

______________________ **5.** value of all final goods and services produced in a country in a year

______________________ **6.** nation with many different ethnic groups

______________________ **7.** denies citizens basic civil rights

______________________ **8.** currency issued by the European Union

______________________ **9.** use of violence and fear to achieve political goals

Notes for Home: Your child learned the vocabulary terms for Chapter 22.
Home Activity: With your child, discuss your family's ethnicity and the countries in which family members or ancestors were born. Identify what economic ties, if any, those countries have with the United States.

Name ______________________ Date __________ **Lesson Review**

Use with Pages 630–633.

Lesson 1: Economic Cooperation

Directions: Read the following descriptions and decide which regional trading bloc each one describes. Write *E* for European Union, *A* for ASEAN, *M* for Mercosur, and *N* for NAFTA. You may use your textbook.

____ **1.** includes Argentina, Brazil, Paraguay, and Uruguay

____ **2.** includes the United States, Mexico, and Canada

____ **3.** includes 15 European nations

____ **4.** includes five Southeast Asian countries

Directions: Answer the following questions on the lines provided.

5. What are three effects of having a global economy?

____

____

____

____

____

____

6. How does a developing country differ from a developed country?

____

____

____

____

____

Notes for Home: Your child learned about global economies and economic cooperation among nations.
Home Activity: With your child, analyze the graph on p. 631. Discuss some of the differences between developing and developed nations. Which countries or regions have the highest and lowest GDP?

Name ______________________ Date ______________ **Chart and Graph Skills**

Use with Pages 634–635.

Interpret Cartograms

A cartogram is a special kind of graph based on a map. A cartogram stretches and bends a nation's boundaries on a map to represent information.

Directions: Read the table below. Then answer the questions about cartograms.

	Area	Population	Population of Largest City	Gross Domestic Product
Yugoslavia	39,499 sq. mi.	11,206,847	1,168,454	$24.3 billion
Rwanda	10,169 sq. mi.	8,154,933	232,733	$3 billion
Ireland	27,136 sq. mi.	3,632,944	1,056,666	$59.9 billion

1. Which of the countries in the table would be the smallest on a cartogram that was based on population? Why?

____

____

2. For which category would Ireland appear as the largest country on a cartogram? Why?

____

____

3. Which country would appear larger based on the population of its largest city: Yugoslavia or Rwanda? Why?

____

____

4. Which country would appear the smallest on a cartogram that was based on area? Why?

____

____

Notes for Home: Your child learned how to interpret cartograms.
Home Activity: With your child, review which cities or countries would be the largest and smallest on a cartogram based on the amount of rainfall they have received.

Name ______________________ Date ____________ **Lesson Review**

Use with Pages 636–641.

Lesson 2: Conflicts of Identity

Directions: Read the following descriptions and decide to which region each refers. Write *Y* for Yugoslavia, *A* for Africa, and *I* for Ireland. Some descriptions may apply to more than one region. Include all regions that fit the description. Then answer the questions that follow.

______ **1.** Issues over identity or ethnicity lead to violence.

______ **2.** Millions of refugees flee or are forced to leave.

______ **3.** Conflicts arise over religion.

______ **4.** Serbs fight Kosovars.

______ **5.** The country is divided geographically.

______ **6.** Hutu fight Tutsi.

______ **7.** The country begins to break apart when the communists lose power.

______ **8.** Catholics fight Protestants.

______ **9.** People engage in ethnic cleansing.

______ **10.** Outside troops are sent in.

11. What are two examples of basic human rights?

____

____

12. Which basic human rights were women denied under the Taliban's rule?

____

____

13. In what ways do you think the governments of developed nations such as the United States can influence a repressive government?

____

____

____

Notes for Home: Your child learned how ethnic, political, and religious differences have led to violence around the world.

Home Activity: With your child, brainstorm ways people can resolve conflicts over identity or ethnicity.

Name ______________________ Date __________ **Lesson Review**

Use with Pages 644–649.

Lesson 3: Political Conflicts and Challenges

Directions: Use the terms in the box to complete each sentence with information from Lesson 3. You may use your textbook.

religion	Oklahoma City	Lockerbie
terrorism	World Trade Center	antiterrorism
Pentagon	Lebanon	Taliban
ethnicity		political beliefs

1. ____________________ can take the form of assassinations, bombings, hijackings, kidnappings, or chemical and germ warfare.

2. People in the military were targeted by terrorists when a car bomb exploded in 1983 at the U.S. embassy in ____________________.

3. In December 1988, an airplane flying over ____________________, Scotland, was destroyed by a terrorist bomb.

4. In April 1995, a car bomb exploded outside the Murrah Federal Building in ____________________, Oklahoma.

5. On the morning of September 11, 2001, hijacked airplanes crashed into the twin towers of the ____________________ in New York City and the ____________________ near Washington, D.C., killing about 3,000 people.

6. Following the terrorist attacks on September 11, Congress passed tougher ____________________ laws to support the fight against terrorism.

7. The United States gathered evidence that the ____________________ government in Afghanistan was protecting the terrorist group responsible for the attacks on September 11.

8. Acts of terrorism are often caused by differences in ____________________, ____________________, or ____________________ among people.

Notes for Home: Your child learned about acts of terrorism and the struggle to fight terrorist attacks around the world.
Home Activity: With your child, brainstorm ways the governments and people around the world can stand up against terrorism. Discuss how the United States has responded to acts of terrorism in the past.

Name ______________________ Date __________

Vocabulary Review

Use with Chapter 22.

Vocabulary Review

Directions: Read each sentence. Then replace the words in italics with the correct vocabulary term from the box and write it on the line provided. Not all words will be used. You may use your glossary.

gross domestic product (GDP)	trade agreement	ethnic cleansing
trading bloc	ethnicity	repressive
euro	multiethnic nation	terrorism

1. Sometimes differences in religion and *shared language, customs, and culture* are factors in war.

   ____

2. Many developed nations have a larger *measure of a nation's wealth* than most developing countries do.

   ____

3. Yugoslavia is an example of a *nation with many different ethnic groups.*

   ____

4. For years, South Africa had a government that was *denying citizens basic civil rights.*

   ____

5. The *group of countries that agree to trade under favorable conditions* formed by the United States, Mexico, and Canada signed the NAFTA agreement in 1994.

   ____

6. After Bosnia declared independence, Slobodan Milosevic encouraged Serb soldiers to carry out a policy of *driving out and sometimes killing the people who do not share the same identity.*

   ____

7. The partnership between the United States, Canada, and Mexico had its roots in a 1989 *understanding that outlines rules about the exchange of goods between countries.*

   ____

Notes for Home: Your child learned the vocabulary terms for Chapter 22.
Home Activity: With your child, read a newspaper article about international trade and banking. What references to trade agreements or trading blocs are made?

Name ______________________ Date ____________ **Vocabulary Preview**

Use with Chapter 23.

Vocabulary Preview

Directions: Match each vocabulary word to its meaning. Write the word on the line provided. Not all words will be used. You may use your glossary.

millennium	greenhouse effect	fossil fuel
megacity	pesticide	nonrenewable resource
demographer	environmentalist	renewable resource
immigration	endangered species	hydroelectric energy
zero population growth	deforestation	geothermal energy
global warming	desertification	space station
carbon dioxide	pollution	satellite
	conservation	

______________ **1.** large satellite in space that serves as a scientific base

______________ **2.** natural resource that can be replaced

______________ **3.** one thousand years

______________ **4.** energy from super-hot water underground

______________ **5.** process of people moving to a new country

______________ **6.** human-made object sent into space

______________ **7.** water power from rapidly flowing rivers or dams

______________ **8.** scientist who studies population trends

______________ **9.** chemical that is used to kill pests

______________ **10.** person who favors taking measures to protect the environment

______________ **11.** animals and plants that could die out

______________ **12.** limiting the use of energy

______________ **13.** city region with 10 million or more people

Notes for Home: Your child learned the vocabulary terms for Chapter 23.
Home Activity: Help your child make flash cards for the vocabulary terms for Chapter 23. Make half of them tonight and the other half tomorrow night. Quiz your child on the definition of each word.

Name ______________________ Date __________ **Lesson Review**

Use with Pages 654–657.

Lesson 1: Population Growth and Change

Directions: Read the following statements. Then write *T* (True) or *F* (False) on the line before each statement. If the answer is false, rewrite the statement to make it true. You may use your textbook.

1. ____ Many of the world's people are moving to rural areas.

____

____

2. ____ Calcutta is one of the richest and most populated cities in the world.

____

____

3. ____ The Industrial Revolution in the late 1800s resulted in an increase in migration from rural areas to urban areas.

____

____

4. ____ Unemployment is high in many developing countries and governments cannot provide good housing and clean water.

____

____

5. ____ Developed countries usually have a higher population growth rate than developing countries.

____

____

6. ____ Many demographers believe that there is a connection between the status of women and a country's population growth rate.

____

____

Notes for Home: Your child learned about trends in the growth and movement of the world's population.
Home Activity: With your child, discuss the effects of population changes on your community. What advantages or disadvantages has your family experienced?

Name ______________________ Date __________

Use with Pages 658–659.

Compare Distribution Maps

Directions: Answer the questions below about distribution maps. You may use your textbook.

1. What is the purpose of distribution maps?

____

____

____

2. What type of symbols do distribution maps use to show the distribution of something across an area?

____

____

____

3. Why might politicians use distribution maps? Why might airlines? Why might city governments?

____

____

____

____

4. Look at the two distribution maps on pp. 658–659. Near what kind of physical feature has much of the world's population settled? On which distribution map did you find this information?

____

____

5. Look at the world population distribution map on p. 658. According to the map key, what symbol represents population? What does a cluster of these symbols indicate about the population of that area?

____

____

Notes for Home: Your child learned how to compare distribution maps.
Home Activity: With your child, discuss how changes in the population density of your community affect the people who live and work there. What effects do population shifts have on local governments and our use of natural resources?

Name ______________________ Date __________ **Lesson Review**

Use with Pages 660–663.

Lesson 2: Earth's Environment

Directions: Complete the cause-and-effect chart with information from this lesson. You may use your textbook.

Cause		Effect
People burn fuels such as coal and oil.	→	
Rachel Carson writes *Silent Spring.*	→	
People begin pressing for laws to protect the environment.	→	
Most nations believe reducing the carbon dioxide they produce will disrupt their economies.	→	
Population increases lead people to cut down forests to plant crops on the land.	→	
Farmers overplant and animals overgraze the land.	→	
Humans do not properly dispose of much waste, such as garbage.	→	

Notes for Home: Your child learned about the causes and effects of damage to Earth's environment.
Home Activity: With your child, set up a recycling system in your home. Create a space to recycle things such as cans, plastic, and newspapers. Decide on a schedule to determine when and how often you will turn in your recyclable products.

Name ______________________ Date ____________ **Lesson Review**

Use with Pages 664–667.

Lesson 3: Energy

Directions: Use the information from Lesson 3 to answer the following questions on the lines provided. You may use your textbook.

1. What are two ways we use fossil fuels?

2. What are two problems related to using fossil fuels to supply energy?

3. What were the causes of the oil crisis of the 1970s?

4. What are the advantages of nuclear power?

5. What are some examples of renewable energy sources? What is the advantage of using these to create energy?

6. How are hydroelectric energy and geothermal energy different?

7. In what ways are scientists trying to solve the world's energy shortage?

Notes for Home: Your child learned about the ways we produce and conserve energy.
Home Activity: With your child, read a newspaper article about energy conservation. What new ways of conservation are discussed?

Name ______________________ Date ____________ **Lesson Review**

Use with Pages 668–671.

Lesson 4: Technology

Directions: Write the events from the box in the chart in the order in which they took place. You may use your textbook.

- Researcher Flossie Wong-Staal helps identify HIV.
- U.S. astronauts Neil Armstrong and Edwin Aldrin walk on the moon.
- UN Secretary-General Kofi Annan urges developed nations to contribute money to help fight AIDS in Africa.
- Desktop computers are introduced for use at home and at work.
- The former Soviet Union launches the *Sputnik I* satellite into space.
- Toolmaking advances from stone to copper.
- Soviet astronaut Yuri Gagarin becomes the first human in space.

1.

2.

3.

4.

5.

6.

7.

Notes for Home: Your child learned about advances in technology and the research scientists continue to conduct.
Home Activity: With your child, make a chart to compare how technology has changed the ways in which people communicate, work, and live from the time you were a child to the present.

Name ______________________ Date ____________ **Vocabulary Review**

Use with Chapter 23.

Vocabulary Review

Directions: Complete each sentence with a vocabulary term from Chapter 23. Write the word on the line provided. Not all words will be used.

1. Some farmers spray their crops with a ______________________ to kill insects.
2. Cutting down forests to create areas to plant crops is called ______________________.
3. Petroleum is a ______________________ because it cannot be easily replaced.
4. Human activities such as burning gasoline in cars produce a gas called ______________________.
5. A gradual increase in the average temperature of Earth's surface is known as ______________________.
6. As a solution to ______________________, people recycle aluminum, paper, and glass.
7. Coal, petroleum, and natural gas are each a ______________________.
8. Tokyo is an example of a ______________________ because more than 10 million people live there.
9. The point at which enough babies are born to balance the number of deaths is called ______________________.
10. Gases trap heat that radiates from Earth's surface in a process called the ______________________.
11. When the topsoil of fertile land becomes loose, dries up, and blows away, the process is called ______________________.
12. Limiting our use of energy, or ______________________, is one solution to the energy crisis.
13. Water power from rivers or dams provides an alternative source of energy called ______________________.

Notes for Home: Your child learned the vocabulary terms for Chapter 23.
Home Activity: Nine vocabulary terms from Chapter 23 were not covered in this exercise. Have your child identify the nine missing terms and use each in an original sentence.

Name ______________________ Date __________

UNIT 8 Project Making Contact

Use with Page 678.

Directions: In a group, design a Web page about the history of communication.

1. Our Web page will feature this communication method or invention:

   ____

2. Description of the method or invention:

   ____

   ____

3. Inventor(s) of this method or invention:

   ______________________ ______________________

4. A time line shows the development of the method or invention through history.

   Earliest use in ___ (year) Additions or improvements in ___, ___ (years) Modern form ___ (year)

5. Pictures we will include to represent our method or invention:

   ______________________ ______________________

   ______________________ ______________________

   ______________________ ______________________

Checklist for Students

_____ We chose a communication method or invention.
_____ We wrote important facts and described it.
_____ We created a time line and pictures showing how it changed over time.
_____ We made a drawing of our Web page.
_____ We presented our Web page to the class.

Notes for Home: Your child learned about the development of communication.
Home Activity: With your child, discuss the different methods of communication used by your family. Which methods have been invented in the last 20 years? What developments in communication do you predict will occur in the next 20 years?

NOTES

NOTES

NOTES

NOTES